Trumpism:

A Cultural Psycho Genesis

with a foreword by
Slavoj Zizek

Michel Valentin, PhD

Trumpekin Pis©2017 by Sarah McClain

Inspired by the famous "*Manneken Pis*" sculpture and fountain in Brussels… The *Manneken Pis* is a landmark small bronze sculpture (61 cm) on a famous plaza in Brussels, depicting a naked little boy urinating into a fountain's basin. It was designed by Hiëronymus Duquesnoy the Elder (from the Netherlands) and put in place in 1618 or 1619. Sarah McClain is a free-lance editor and cartoonist living in Missoula, Montana.

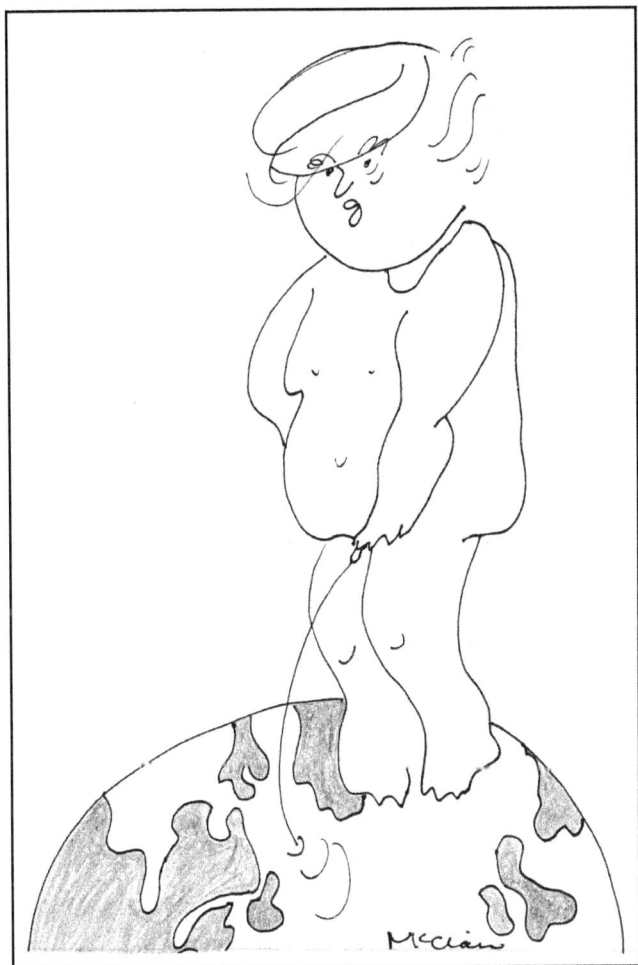

EPIS Press
2026 S 9th W, #4
Missoula, MT 59801 USA
epispublishing1@gmail.com
episworldwide.com
episeducation.com
episjournal.com

Printed in the United States of America

Library of Congress Cataloging-In-Publication Data
1. Trump 2. Critical Theory 3.Cultural Psychoanalysis
4. Social Theory 5. Slavoj Zizek 6.Postmodern Populism
7. Capitalism I. Title

Cover art: *Trumpekin Pis*©2017 by Sarah McClain

Alternate cover photo-composit: *Icarus? No, Donald with his golden parachute!—Alan Graham Mcquillan, ARPS Associate, photographer living in Missoula, Montana—www.alanmcquillan.com

Production Manager: Tia Taylor
ISBN: 978-1-943332-17-5
Library of Congress Control Number: 2018941397

The Lost Souls of Mid-America and The Braggadocio of Manhattan

Michel VALENTIN

foreword Slavoj Zizek

Table of Contents

Preface

I am pleased to introduce the seminal text for our new book series focusing on psychoanalytic and phenomenological perspectives concerning social, political, and cultural phenomena in the United States and Europe. The instant text, Trumpism: A Cultural Psycho Genesis, is such an analysis of the political and cultural background within which Trumpism has become a phenomenon. In this text, the author, Professor Michel Valentin, by way of prolegomena, explores a new road for those interested in political struggle, freedom, and reform. This is the first of three texts, a trifecta of works, that together offer new semiological, psychoanalytic, and critical perspective on the changing landscape of American life.

Dr. Kevin Boileau
Executive Editor
EPIS Press
Existential Psychoanalytic Institute & Society

Foreword

There is something missing in the overflow of essays on Donald Trump. These essays mostly focus on the personality of Trump, making fun of him with a dose of liberal arrogance, they play the simplistic cards of economy (blue collar workers as the losers of capitalist globalization), or use old terms like "Fascism" to avoid concrete analysis. What is missing is a more detailed analysis of the complex political and ideological background of the Trump phenomenon, a demonstration of how this phenomenon is not an eccentricity, how it grew out of the mainstream of the American politics. This is what Michel Valentin, in his beautifully written *The Lost Souls of Mid-America and the Braggadocio of Manhattan*, does. Combining irony and sarcasm with cold rational analysis, political science with psychoanalysis, Valentin deploys the contours of what is effectively a new politico-ideological formation, a new form of American "national-capitalist-populism." His book is indispensable for all of us who want to understand where our society is moving, as well as to grasp the dangers and, perhaps, new chances for emancipatory struggle that the Trump phenomenon is opening.

Slavoj Zizek
Hegelian philosopher, Lacanian psychoanalyst, political activist, socio-political and cultural critique author of numerous books

Introduction

"No need to believe in a truth to sustain it nor to love a period to justify it; every principle being demonstrable and every event legitimate. The sum of phenomena—whether fruits of the mind or of time— can be embraced or denied according to our mood of the moment: arguments, proceeding from our rigor or from our whims, are of equal weight on each point. Nothing is indefensible—from the absurdist proposition to the most monstrous crime."[1]

Instead of confronting the insidious reality of capitalism, its contradictions, insurmountable paradoxes, and implacable globalization, which today define and structure the totality of human civilization, many of our fellow citizens, animated by fantasy and fear, find sentimental solace and affective shelter in extreme religious expression, and/or in paranoia-based politics. Instead of questioning the competitive individualism, made ubiquitous by a neo-liberal economic system, or addressing the dire, capitalist hyper-reality of High-Tech's virtual dimension, both of which de-humanize us a little more every day, many of our nationals prefer to attack the Media, Higher-Education, and the Government, whom they see as irremediably "traitorously liberal," "ungodly" and secular, or "radically leftist," that is to say, undependable, dispendious, and therefore dispensable. These two (relatively) new types of religious and socio-financial rebellions (one anti-federalist and anti-governmental, the other anti-taxation and anti-Wall Street) constitute the bifurcated form of what political scientists vaguely defined as "modern populism," i.e. an apolitical way of doing politics, or, as some analysts claim, the end of politics as such.2

Are these "rebellious" fellow-Americans poor actors performing a cynical act of ultimate resistance via the negative, against the "inhuman order" which J.P. Sartre called the "*pratico-inerte*," or are they the grass-roots "expressionist *porte-paroles*" of a popular discontent, disbelief, cynicism and disgust, in an era of dis-engagement of the centralized rule of the nation-state, itself the result of the rhizome-like diffusion and propagation of multinational capital? Are our conscious American populist participants in the evolution of the body-politic instinctually following Jean Baudrillard when he said that, ultimately, a new form of socialism will emerge from the death of the social stung by the virulent virus of market economy gone viral, in the same way as renewed, extreme religious expressions emerged after "the death of God" (Nietzsche), or are they merely hypnotized actors in the very devolution of society?3 Are they anticipating the radical transformation of the body-politic via a new, anti-Establishment form of postmodern, populist socialism, or are they mindlessly rehearsing its dramatic disappearance? Are they forerunners announcing "*the emergences of something that cannot be integrated into the existing ideological frameworks, signs of the New the path-breaking character of which is attested by the very fact that they do not know what they are signs of and therefore often take refuge in the language of the past…"*[4], or are they just puppets and fools, riding the new wave of prejudices sweeping across the West?

Postmodern Populism

It is, of course, too early to draw a conclusion. One thing is sure though. Many Americans hesitate between the acknowledgment of the apocalyptic emptiness of the world (anticipated by the Millenarian tradition of many Evangelist or Baptist Churches) and the recognition of the general emptiness of life (fed by material over-indulgence or falling expectations). Although they have been seduced by, or have bought into the individualist ideology of self-contentment and self-enrichment propagated by the neo-capitalist System of production and consumption, they feel deeply anxious about the destruction of morality and ethical restraints (of all "*retenues*") favored by the neo-capitalist System. This existential and ontological doubt and tug-of-war leaves them unable to track the sources of their malaise, examine them, and go beyond appearances in order to draw rational and informed conclusions. We will define the System as the complex nexus of laws, practices, impositions and permissions, cultural mores, advertising, entertainment materials, and consumerist habits, which structure and streamline cultures, citizens, and consumers; informing, reforming, (and deforming) them.

In their defense, too many Americans have been shortchanged by a deficient mass-educational system that does not develop the significant critical capacity necessary to see clearly through the System's ideology, to recognize who and what are their true enemies. They have forgotten, or were never told, their past history. The narrative of rebellious commoners uniting together over two centuries, to battle illiberal and repressive forces such as the colonialism of the British monarchy, feudal slavery, Jim Crow laws, the 1900s Robber Barons, Nazism, different movements of bigotry, and waves imperialist corporate abuse. High-Schools had the tendency to deliver a "History of the American People" which was biased, partial, and oblivious to the plight of Native Americans. In many ways the birth and vicissitudes of the American, collective dream of "equality, fairness, and justice for all" parallel the other great Western dream, the French revolutionary ideals of "*liberté, égalité, fraternité.*"

Not only have the Primary and Secondary schools failed the American people, consumerism and capitalist globalization are re-defining Higher-Education along the paradigms and values of the "free-market," and its underpinning of corporate, utilitarian logic. That is to say, it has become harder and harder for people to distinguish not only between "being" and "non-being," (aggravating psycho-sexual traumas and palliative addictions), but between fact and fiction, reality and its representation, fake-news and news. The relative freedom from the religious, metaphysical or political certainties that used to beset their elders as late as the 1930s, the "end-of-history triumphalism" of the millennials' age did not translate for them into a more creative freedom, or an open, although hopeful, uncertainty. Instead, they found themselves in the thrall of the System, in the clutches of a petit-bourgeois and hedonist operative or functional disorder, i.e. the logic of the market, whose diktats now appear as strong as natural laws (from which nobody seems able to disentangle themselves). It is a System seemingly without teleology or over-arching destiny; a machinery of market-means without ends—except for the goals to reproduce itself indefinitely, and to produce surplus-value for a minority at the top.

The System no longer permits them to obtain the discriminating critical knowledge necessary to distinguish between the Imaginary and the Symbolic dimensions, something which is now finally alarming many state lawmakers, a paradoxical situation since many of these politicos adopted (and still follow) a laissez-faire attitude and policy when confronted by the erosive pressures on the place and study of the Humanities in Secondary and Higher-Education exerted by the mercantile and utilitarian logic of the market.[5] Moreover, these politicos and pundits were (and are still) willing accomplices in the public de-funding of Higher-Ed. They are tacitly or actively engaged in the reduction of the social benefits of taxation and state investments, which used to guarantee a free (in Europe), or subsidized and affordable university education, and its replacement by a privately funded system. This reduction in the name of the private translates into a public re-education of citizens into buyers. The "unmaking of many public universities" and their brutal replacement by bodies functioning likes companies, widens the rift already existing between the complex culture of spirit and intellect (thought or thinking), the expansive cultivation of knowledge (sciences), and the transmission of skills and acquisition of information (technology). Although urgently needed in an increasingly lost and ignorant society (in spite of the protests voiced by many proponents of the so-called Social Media and Info-Society), the devolution of Higher-Ed tends to make spiritual and critical thinking developed by print-culture obsolete.

Students have become consumers and administrators petty C.E.O.s or "line-managers." Everywhere in the West, and especially in the U.S., economists and would-be C.E.O.s have taken over the administration of most universities and colleges. The consequences are that the critical, higher-thinking dimension, which used to characterize the "special nature" of a humanist education is de-valued, made obsolete or irrelevant; to be replaced by a skill-based type of know-how geared to the direct needs of an information-based economy, and the labor needs of the market-workforce, as the British example illustrates:

> *"When the education secretary, Charles Clarke (giving an example, it seems, of managerial*

deadwood), recently stated that medieval historians were all right "for ornamental purposes but there is no reason for the state to pay for them," suggesting that money should go instead to subjects of "clear usefulness."[6]

Postmodern populism is, therefore, a by-product of the System and its educational policy—or lack thereof.

Populist confusion also shows that the difference between real events and imagined ones is more a difference in degree than in kind, especially in a postmodern society whose referents have become more and more hyper-real and hyper-virtual (Jean Baudrillard's definition of the words[7]), opening the door for the unchecked, all-pervasive reign of the Imaginary (Lacanian meaning).

Many of our fellow-citizens are broken pieces of what, once, they were; of what, once, they had. They are the lost souls of postmodern contemporary society; they do not know who they are any longer. They do not know what they are, what they have, or where they are; if what they possess makes them whom they are. They do not know what belongs to them anymore, or to whom or what they belong. Their minds sedimented by mental filters (prejudices, biases, fixed ideas, fears…) they are neither able to think ontologically about their lives, nor capable of fathoming their ontic dimension. Their spiritual and transcendental dimension has often been hijacked by the mercantilist pseudo-religions of Mega Churches and philistine TV Evangelists. Threatened by downward mobility (which makes them petit-bourgeois in danger of pauperization), they swim in the sea of debt and mass-consumption that their country, America, has become. The consumerism they still enjoy is made affordable by the paltry salaries imposed on the proletariat of "developing" countries, the same countries whose socialist experiments the capitalist Occident has never allowed to succeed (China excepted, but which power can force China into anything?). In their acquiescent eyes, these foreign countries with their intrusively competitive and complacently ultra-diligent workers or invasive migrants constitute the "otherness" their presidential candidate Donald Trump was quick to prey upon and demonize during his campaign. Their distracted indifference towards immigrants (never mind the geography of the immigrants' provenance) suddenly turned to militant malevolence. Having lost any moral compass, many in our population are in danger of becoming a mob of bigots (i.e. a population supporting an aggressively racist populism). They navigate haphazardly, untrusting of what is left of beacons, lights and buoys. They all share a pervasive resentment that is susceptible to being enlisted as "emotional fuel" for manipulative, political projects.

They tread water in a hedonist-utilitarian and hyper-individualist world, where "dog eats dog," an economic morass of commodification, "a soup of

signs" of all sorts, of laws, regulations and count-
er-regulations, of non-stop injunctions to enjoy
and buy things, and prohibitions of certain forms
of enjoyment; a propaganda propagating nothing
and everything; a Sargasso sea of contradictory
messages drifting everywhere in "virtual digital
bottles," with pornographic images saturating the
currents, unfurling themselves like hydras and
jelly-fish, floating in suspended animation—exacerbating desire, while pre-empting its materiality
by hyper-realizing/hyper-virtualizing it; hate-filled
texts with emoticons brought ashore by the tem-
pestuous waves of Social Media, amid drifting
archipelagoes of broken dreams, filled with the
flotsam of derelict thoughts and beliefs, the relics
of the burnt-out shells of factories, thwarted hopes,
hardship and pollution of all kinds …, "*the huddled
masses… of tempest-tost junk… and the wretched
refuse of [our] teeming shores*," cast into the middle
of the sea…, giving to Emma Lazarus' poem a tragic, ironic twist.[8] For many of them, globalization
means international trade (which it principally is!),
i.e. a game they do not control or always understand, except that it translates for them into a ruth-
less, constraining, cut-throat competition, at best
putting a damper on their benefits and pensions, at
worst costing them their jobs (outsourcing).

Globalization does not necessarily mean open-end-
ed and multicultural post-nationalism, exciting
and enlightened trans-nationalism, informed
and aware nomadism, or even cultural hybridity,

and jet-setting across political boundaries, states, cultures and ethnic territories; a pure, yuppie-like *jouissance* of unlimited boundaries, as many ads brazenly display in glossy magazines. Globalization is first and foremost the world-wide governance of a new form of capital intimately allied to High-Tech instrumentalization and postmodern tele-communications and networks (the Web). It is the world-wide rule of the "*pensée unique*" (French expression encapsulating the intimate alliance between "free-market" ideology, laissez-faire-lais-sez-passer, and deregulation), of the international, fluid predominance of fluxes and flows of finance, systems experts, financial jack-of-all-trades, products, goods, commodities, and workers across the globe, with the aim and the result of producing a unified global market obeying the laws and drive (Lacanian meaning) of capital. The logical aim of globalization's outsourcing is the satellization of all production and finances into a global sphere, displacing or replacing the original, physical sphere, or placated it like a veil or ghostly membrane. For many Americans, globalization is an empty word, inciting in them envy, resentment, and anxiety—especially when we know that most Americans are tongue-tied (mono-lingual—another failure of the educational system) and do not possess a passport. Although, the world-over, globalization has lifted hundreds of millions out of poverty and allowed other millions to join the middle-class, the ideology and reality of globalization has jump-started anti-egalitarianism and xenophobia, while seriously exacerbating socio-economic inequality and accelerating an ominous process of problematic environmental changes which maybe already beyond control.[9]

Our unfortunate countrymen are victims of a de-sublimation of the social, of the violence of the capitalist state's assaults on anything smacking of proletarian social life, of public spaces (what used to be part of the "commons" has been privatized, or has to be locally regained, here and there, via the application of "eminent domain policies").[10] Herbert Marcuse finds the causes of the de-sublimation of the social in a socio-political order re-defined by the reign of technology, mass-consumption, and the "*Infontainment*" industry, producing, curiously enough, citizens no longer "*haunted by father images*," but obsessed by the need for a "group mutual identification": peers, gang leaders, stars, sport heroes, gangsters…[11] These icons are not transcendental but provide what the sociologist Michel Maffesoli call "*l'être-en-semble*" ("*being-togetherness*"), i.e. a cure against individualized loneliness and anxiety.

Postmodern capitalism has accelerated the loss of the signifiers of the traditional "group transcendence" (workers, blue-collars, farmers, citizens…)—a loss welcomed by many political philistines on the right and the left. But these icons still live in the public mind as a sort of melancholic reminder or left-overs. Is this why all candidates of the recent Presidential campaign, except for

Donald Trump, and Bernie Sanders of course, very rarely mentioned the expression "working class," preferring instead to use the expression "middle-class?" It is interesting to note that, on February 24, 2017, during a speech delivered to a conservative convention, Donald Trump spoke of the Democratic candidate, Bernie Sanders, in complimentary terms (something rare indeed), even claiming that many Sanders' supporters voted for him during the Presidential election. Both, from opposite ends of the political spectrum, strived, via their anti-political establishment stand to unseat the Washington political elites and give back to the people, at least nominally, the political power hijacked by the top of the economic and political pyramid, the 1% who control the US economy. The irony, lost on his supporters, is that, although a New-Yorker and not a Washingtonian, Donald Trump is part of this economic elite, which gives to his political discourses a perverse, Imaginary dimension.

Many Trump supporters are casualties of an increasingly deracinated state, which can no longer defend or guarantee the forms of collective life, as such, which are the pre-conditions (and limits) of politics.[12] Their lives are increasingly subjected to impersonal, global forces, which de-subjectify and ob-jectify them—something important that will be analyzed further. If this situation endures, it will doom political life in the long run. It is perhaps why, already, postmodern populism conjures up the spirit of fascism, the return of the repressed of modern history.

Postmodern populism is the transformation of the proletariat after the impact of consumerism and individualism. Contrary to the proletariat who used to have a class consciousness and pride, and who used to "get even" (fighting back against their oppressors), today's populists have an inferiority complex and are eaten inside by what Nietzsche used to call "resentment."

They are often called by the intellectual, artistic, academic or political elites, red-necks, losers, blue-collar workers, white trash... Mixing qualitative expletives with quantitative invectives, societal ignorance with class-arrogance, Bostonian moguls, New-Yorker tycoons, Washingtonian plutocrats, or Hollywoodian barons or actors nicknamed them "waste people," "undesirable Southern whites," "the poor," "the rubbish," "mudsills," "the waste," "trailer-trash," "grits," "Walmart shoppers," "Evangelist morons..."[13] After the 1860s, many fled the poverty of a defeated South and "went West," where they came to be known as "copperheads," because of their Confederate sympathies. Already anti-Washingtonian and anti-Federalist, they were fierce Independents (this is why the Frontier attracted them), or anti-Republican State-Rightists (obviously, the Republican Party has since changed). Do our new populists, in a strange way, carry on (and sometimes "act out") the rebellious and irredentist tradition of the "copperhead mentality" characteristic of many rural or sparsely populated States, a space where God and the land (nature) function as a redemptive place? Most "Red States," by the way, are located in the South or the West.[14]

The Liberals, whom they hate in return, lambasted them as "white men" (the worst insult in certain Politically Correct Democratic circles), or "*deplorables*" (Hillary Clinton)—hence their "illiberalism."[15] Their anti-liberalism, mixed with their anti-intellectualism and anti-elitism (iconized by their hatred for "Ivy-Leaguers"), is an inchoate, quasi-instinctive response to what they perceive as their total social and political alienation from urban civilization, from society, and from the System at large. Their plight and sorrows can be also understood as a direct indictment of the basic failure of the American mass education system (only 33 percent of young Americans graduated from college in the Spring of 2017.) This is why their language and culture make them stand apart, from the Great Lakes to the Gulf of Mexico (from Fargo to Mobile): "*Given the resilience of the white trash slur, rural working-class whites hardly needed liberal lingo to feel alienated.*"[16] This is why many lower-class whites love candidates who say aloud in public what they speak about amongst themselves with anger and resentment,[17] while manhandling the English language: "*Sarah Palin's Fargoesque accent made her tortured speech patterns sound even worse. Former TV talk show host Dick Cavett wrote a scathing satirical piece in which he dubbed*

her a "serial syntax killer" whose high school English department deserved to be draped in black."[18]
When asked what they prefer in him, Donald Trump's supporters mention his raw honesty and the way he speaks his mind—as if he were reading their minds, however crude or uninformed their thoughts are. As Nancy Isenberg writes in her very thoughtful study on white trash and class in America, Donald Trump loudly broadcast, during his campaign, his love of "the poorly educated." Reversing the social opprobrium projected upon them by the Liberals and the Establishment, the new populists proudly wear, like a tattoo, the "white trash label," pinned upon them as a badge of honor.

Lo and behold, there are also middle-class voters and educated people among the new "national populists," and many a woman; believers in rugged individualism, independents, and "tea-partiers." There are also many small businessmen and women, and people of color—bourgeois and petit-bourgeois. They do not understand "Black Lives Matter" because they feel that their own lives are slowly disintegrating and nobody seems to care. This is why they unwittingly answered back with "White Lives Matter" protests—something devilishly prepared by the provocative Media statements of the ex-Mayor of New York and manipulator-extraordinaire Rudy Giuliani, who, throwing fuel on the fire, cynically accused "Black Lives Matter" activists of racism by excluding all other "colors."

Unemployment, underemployment, and a series of menial jobs allow these disgruntled, frustrated masses to keep up some appearances. But how long can they keep up the pretense and escape their conditions? Alcoholism, angst, drugs, juvenile lawlessness, violence, uns, suicide…, none constitutes a politics, nor guarantees a cure.[19] These solutions of despair take their toll and levy their pound of flesh. The youngest among them can escape by enlisting, going to war, and then using the G.I. Bill, going to college—providing they have enough fortitude. But what about the others?

They do not turn their economic rage on the information age or the "new economy" as such. They turn their fear of the future on the invading others whose own *jouissance*[20] they think threatens theirs by taking their jobs and displacing their values; against the diffuse external threat, they want the politics of the stick, a super-military and a Wall barring the intrusion of a "threatening South" (Anglos/Yankees against Latinos). This new anti-immigration and anti-foreigner virulence which characterizes Western postmodern populisms is paradoxically an unintentional by-product of commercial globalization. Its consequences are serious, because beyond its racist aspects, it fundamentally disrupts the complex circuitry of affects and effects (product of the Enlightenment's progressist socio-cultural gains) leading from unity and multiplicity, and then followed by the re-integrative return of multiplicity into unity. This

feed-back-loop has, for better or worse, produced—and incidentally stabilized, the modern nation-state. Today, globalization (strangely enough,
in a manner akin to what "identity politics" have
done to politics) has subdivided unified abstract, or
material conceptions of humanity into atomized,
competing, insular and irredentist quasi-monads
at odds with each other. Global competition with
the other, and mass-intrusion of poor emigrants
from the South, which is first and foremost a place
of another speech, of other languages (threatening "mono-lingualism"), have nurtured fear and
paranoia.

Since globalization is often associated with, or
demands a certain level of education (experts,
technocrats, "*décideurs*," international "mov-
ers-and-shakers..."), our anxious citizens direct
their anger and their emotional frustration into irrational attacks on the intellectuals or liberals they
believe to be responsible for their economic and
emotional problems. Their politics is not conservative. It is revisionist at best, reactionary at worst.

They see themselves as victims, passive recipients
of all kinds of aggressions, which explains why they
stick to their guns, in more ways than one. They
feel that they are real losers—the worst thing in
a society which glorifies economic success, individualism and winners.[21] Their economic populist
passions bizarrely spare or forgive the *banksters*. Is
it because America has always shown a weakness
for "high-stake rollers?" For financial dare-devils

who defy the System and succeed? Or is it that members of the socio-economic elite have also become populists? Or is it because populists, too, worship money?

The answer to this question is simpler.

Deep inside, America has always co-opted bad guys who fought off the System (i.e. effete and corrupt civilization, government, etc.)—hence her fascination with Western gun shooters, Depression era mobsters, film noir gangsters, "tough self-made men" like Mafiosi. "Mafioso" means "made man" (self-made man), dramatically epitomizing a type of "rugged individualism making it at all costs." America likes people who elevated themselves above the fray by their own bootstraps via the power of their fists, the accuracy of their shooting ability, or their indomitable shark-like appetites. In a society entirely defined by the economy and the financial status of its entrepreneurs and politicians, evil, or at least badness, is understood as the necessary consequence of people, who, economically left behind, want revenge. The brazen, unapologetic, vulgar, gaudy Trump is the poor man's revenge; the common man's repressed fantasy of "getting even." They want their "big Kahuna," or "big Cheese" to run the show (their show?); their "big Shot" to call the shots (their shots?); a plutocrat for the populace.

They feel that the American dream has abandoned them, that the System is making fun of them, that

the very rich, whom they envy, are laughing at
them all the way to the bank. They feel the gays
have more rights than they, that the government
has abandoned them while pandering to the needs
of the (irresponsible) poor, the "people of color,"
"the brown ones," the criminals, the deviants, the
illegal immigrants, the "traitors," "slackers," and
"cowards;" those "who do not pay taxes." Although
they have been "massified" by the System They feel
that the Democratic party has moved on to issues
of race, gay rights, global warming, and globalization, while leaving them behind, and that the
identity politics the Party (that used to be "theirs")
seemingly espouses, has left them behind. The
Democrats have followed (and also initiated) a Republican retreat from the New Deal legacy, which
started in the 1980s (which the neo-cons called a
roll-back movement or re-conquest). This legacy
was based on a pragmatic alliance between the capitalist forces and the forces of production, between
Wall Street and Main Street; supported by factory
workers, unions, small businesses, small shop-
keepers and small farmers. The Democratic Party
started to abandon its own populist connections
after President Clinton's election. It ignored the
fact that the postindustrial wasteland of the North-
East and the Upper Middle-West was the site of a
meaningful social and political discontent. Hillary
Clinton thought that by throwing out her net wide
and far, she would catch, in the same move, LBGTs,
Blacks and Latinos, emigrants, working women,
and students with loans…, and at the same time,

break the "glass ceiling." Democrats were too quick to replace their "leftist-liberal stand" with a Politically Correct stance, and espouse the tenets of the new financial capitalism as the surest route to prosperity, mass-employment and consumerism: efficiency, speed, concentration, instant monetization, High-Tech, computerization, and robotics. While private funding and financial contributions oil the cogs and wheels of the political machine, flooding the whole electoral system, and changing its nature, Democratic Party pundits shifted their political focus onto a new constituency made up of affluent, college-educated whites cultivating identity politics, feminists, cultural minorities, and environmentalists, i.e. white-collar workers, egg-heads, technocrats; abandoning the blue-collar class and the economically under-privileged whom they consider to be a dwindling category.

The "lost souls" are not totally to blame for their naivety. It is true that the price paid by identity politics is class-politics. Issues of class have become pre-empted by issues of identity—especially sexual identity, as if America's most pressing problem was sex (perhaps it is, in a certain uncanny way). Instead of radical economic policies (represented by Bernie Sanders—hence his vast appeal—something which scared Democratic politicos) and courageous, political economic visions, the Democrats have encouraged, at all levels of society, a Political Correctness whose excessive and, at times, grotesque omnipresence have alienated many

American workers, black and white, female and male. How many votes did the ridiculous "bathroom problems" of North Carolina cause the Democratic Party to lose? Wooing the woes of a minute minority of loo-goers does not make a national politics. This may partly explain why 53% of white females voted for Donald Trump, and also why 47% of all voters abstained from casting a ballot.[22]

Americans were all raised with the notion that if one worked hard in life, it would pay off and one would make it. Well, that doesn't hold true anymore. People are working hard (too hard, often, and holding several jobs to make both ends meet) and many of them are not making it. Their parents were not raised with the same lack of expectations. There used to be an incredible hope for the future. In fact, all parenting is today an all-out war to ensure one's child has a good place at the consumerist banquet-table. But parents today know full well there isn't room anymore at the table for everyone. They confusedly think that, actually, there are things that society as a whole could do that would make "America great again," although they refuse to radically act on it. Trump is but a palliative. America put a man on the Moon (with all the ensuing economic and technical spin-offs) when America was dreaming big dreams, and, by golly, these dreams were coming true: equal rights, desegregation, women's rights and equality…, the "Great Society." But now people sense that everybody has stopped dreaming "Big" and many citizens have lost hope for an exciting future. And as parents they know this all too well. Today's parenting is based upon a resigned fear of the future. Not the type of hope-for-the-future and progress that we were all raised with—hence, the examples of very bizarre childrearing techniques, and competition between parents. Child-rearing today involves a lot of lying to children about the future, a future that will be worse than it is today.

A great majority of Americans are unaware of the enormity and villainy of what is being done to them by the masters of the System and their political lackeys. Their lack of critical education makes them unaware that their sense of self is not only highly contextualized (something common to every humans), but also trapped by a social Imaginary which limits the way they are able to imagine the whole of society and find the true causes and culprits for their increasingly dysfunctional lives. They can fantasize all the way they want, video-games and hyper-virtual alternate realities are there to help them out, but essentially, all this Imaginary freedom does not translate into any genuine, political reality or even utopian dream. They can play all the exotic planet video-games and watch all the alien movies they can, because nothing else will happen in their lives; not because the System makes it impossible (in fact the possibilities of an unleashed capitalism are endless) but because the System has been locked up by politicos and financiers who can no longer dream, who cannot think further than the limits of their off-shore bank accounts.[23] This is why the Kennedy's 60s were more innovative, promise-laden, and utopian than our 2010s. This is why our fellow American populists mimetically (following the big guys' example) disengage their reason from their authentic self and cannot think holistically or look further than the end of their noses.

This is why they want to believe in a "Savior" who is also a common-sense guy like themselves. Not only someone who gives it to them straight, as it were; who tells them lies they like (who cares since everybody is lying?) or want to believe;[24] but also someone who transcends their social situation and status. Trump knows how to "work the angles," providing not only the hat but also the rabbit, but without the magic (he is a "no-nonsense guy" after all). Their suspension of disbelief, entertained by Hollywood movies, works in Donald Trump's favor. His political discourses (campaign addresses) are highly socially symbolic and performative, emotive acts. They are not descriptive in the traditional, realist sense of the word, but reactive, although their plausibility is "descriptive;" a term borrowed from Roland Barthes' semiotics of discourse analysis which characterizes the relation of a certain type of emotive/performative discourse to the discourse of reality. Trump's speech-effects have nothing to do with reality itself—or very little.[25] At least his lies awakened emotions and brought back to politics a passion that had disappeared. Of course, "the

Savior" has savoir-faire and his discourse is savory to their ears. He succeeded in using the worn-out demagogic, but still effective, trick of personifying "the American people" as some entity that has a voice and a will (a perversion of Jean-Jacques Rousseau's famous "*volonté générale*"—popular will) that he is incarnating. He persuaded many Americans that he is embodying their voice, opinions, and feelings, and that anybody who speaks against him speaks against them, and consequently, is their enemy—the enemy of the American people. This curious "state of political affairs" corresponds to the ultimate stage of the evolution of the Marxist conception of "false consciousness" and "ideology." We can no longer merely say that ideology produces (and is the result of) a "false consciousness; i.e. an illusory representation of "the way things are," or of "the way we are," because "postmodern reality" has itself became "ideological; it has become symptomatic. The behavior of individuals has become the symptomatic expression of an inherently ideological reality:

" 'Ideological' is a social reality whose very existence implies the non-knowledge of its participants in its essence—*that is, the social effectivity, the very reproduction of which implies that the individuals 'do not know what they are doing.'* **'Ideological' is not 'the false consciousness' of a (social) being but this being itself in so far as it is supported by 'false consciousness.'**[26]

Trump Extreme-Right Capitalism

In spite of its unorthodoxy and unpredictability, and the possibility that President Bush may be the last Republican President Representative of what the Republican Party stood for, Trump's Presidency is well contained within the limits of the historical movement which has been characterizing the American Right since the Reagan era.

From the 1970s onwards, the Republican Party agenda has been to roll back the progressive gains and socio-economic advantages acquired by the American working-class and laid out during the socio-political, cultural and economic battles of the 60s and 70s. Some rightists were bent on rejecting any measures they considered to be promoting/advocating socio-economic equality. Some even wanted to go back as far as President Roosevelt's New Deal, trying to roll back the reforms which saved the country from utter chaos. But the roots of this peculiar, anti-democratic, elitist, right-wing, ultra-conservatism go back further in time.

The Duke University historian Nancy MacLean explains in *Democracy in Chains: The Deep History of the Radical Right's Stealth Plan for America*, how modern right-wing conspirators, such as the Koch brothers and their followers, found their inspiration for their plutocratic conspiracy in the writings of John Calhoun, a 19th century, Yale-educated,

South-Carolina plantation and slave-owner who became a politician, a US Senator and a Vice-President (his political career spans 40 years—from 1810 to 1850). Our modern and postmodern plutocrats directly borrowed from Calhoun's theories the "moral right" (and duty) of the upper-class (the "makers" and "tax producers" of society, i.e. those who own the means of production and give work to the populace—slaves included), to lord it over the people (i.e. "the takers" or "tax consumers") and impose its political will over the majority, in order to prevent the masses from taking over or acting collectively.

Today's super-rich owners of capital publicly espouse and publicly spout the same principles. They depict "*the masses—particularly common workers and poor people—as irresponsible, selfish moochers, either unable to unwilling to be producers. Disdainfully portrayed as always looking for handouts from government and corporate chieftains, America's commoners are cast as nuisances who must be restrained by law from using their numerical majority to interfere in any way with the "liberty" of the nation's wealth creators.*"[27]

Different conservative movements allied with multibillionaires such as Charles and David Koch, and the Mercer, DeVose and Adelson families…, together with undisclosed multinational corporations have for decades, "*mounted a sneaky, slow motion coup of attrition, moving methodically from one political venue to another, donning multiple*

organizational guises to strike down a law here,
reverse a public policy there, demonize "others,"
and ambush progressive groups all along the way.
Consequently, over decades, the essential American
idea that "we're all in this together" has been steadily
losing out to a diametrically opposed idea: "each of
us is on our own... This bleak outlook is even recog-
nized as a formal political doctrine: selfish individ-
ualism. Basically an ethic of greed, this "philosophy"
is being advanced by a plutocratic elite that insists
that the role of the government is not to promote our
common interests and do the will of the majority,
but to protect the property and accumulated wealth
of moneyed individuals from the rest of us. They are
anti-tax, anti-regulation, anti-union, anti-majority
radicals."[28] They have made parroting disciples
such as Senator Mitch McConnell, Republican
Paul Ryan, or blind followers such as tea-party
proselytizers, doctrinaires of right-wing talk-
shows, wealth-creators, Big Spenders, prosperity
producers, giants of industry, finance or "high-tech
start-ups which made it", all spouting the virtues of
laisser-faire/laisser-passer (supply-side) economics,
self-made men and women. They are persuaded
that they are superior to the norm (Socio-Dar-
winism), and should therefore control the Nation's
political, economic and social destiny by divesting
the public sector and favor capital accumulation.
They are the financial "winners" dictating to the
poor "losers" what liberty should be.

To go back to the contemporaneity of this

ultra-conservative movement we could cautiously date the beginning of the modern form of this right-wing, reactionary (meaning a policy of "going back in time" in matters of state-business-working-class relationships) Republicanism (nothing to do with the Republican Party of the 19th century) to the end of WWII. The post WWII Republican "war of socio-political and ideological re-conquest" started with The Mont Pelerin Society (ironic title semiotically mixing a Pilgrim's Progress/places and journeys of pilgrimage/proselytizing/Christianity/renewals of vows/faith revivals…), which was an international, neoliberal (European meaning, of course) organization founded on April 10 1947, at a conference in Switzerland, by Friedrich Hayek—which is not surprising. The ideology (tactics, methodology, and strategy) of this loose organization was to combat what they perceived to be the unbearable and very limiting state control over socio-economic matters (via planning and intervention), especially the controls of Marxist or Keynesian obedience. Its primary goal was to fight Marxist, communist, and socialist influences and ideas which it considered to be the mortal enemy. Its ideology, of course, was framed by the Cold War bi-polar struggle and its fear of being forced to deal with a post-Bandung-Conference-Third-World (1955) under communist influence. The Mont Pelerin Society aimed at being a platform for what it considered to be a counter-propaganda against Communist propaganda, allowing the "free exchange" of ideas promoting and defending the

Western style "free-market" between like-minded scholars. Its goal was the strengthening of the basic principles and practice (capitalist praxis) of a "free-market-economy" supposed to give birth to a "free society," as well as the pragmatic study (nothing philosophically deep, of course) of the workings, virtues, superiority and problems-to-be-fixed of market-oriented economic systems. In its ranks were economists, philosophers, historians, intellectuals, businessmen, and other persons of influence committed to the defense of economic, private (meaning individual/personal), and political freedoms in society. In fact, although they made sure to keep a certain distance from Senator McCarthy's methods, they basically never publically took a stand against him. Its founders included the Austrian School of Economics' gurus Friedrich Hayek and Ludwig von Mises, Karl Popper, Frank Knight (University of Chicago), George Stigler, and Milton Friedman, most of whom became the pillars and heralds of Republican American values in the 60s and 70s until today. They were all proponents of a fierce individualism, strong anti-socialism, and economic laissez-faire-laissez-passer (anti-statist deregulations). To those think-tankers and pedagogues must be added, especially, the libertarian (and basically anti-democratic) economist James Buchanan (Nobel Prize), leader of the so-called "Virginia School of economics."

The Mont Pelerin society advocated freedom of expression (limited of course, in spite of its own denegation), free-market economic policies, and the political values of a democratic, open society. Although advocating Media freedom, The Mont Pelerin Society already showed the same ambivalence as Donald Trump towards what they believed to be the Liberal or Leftist biases of the printed press and the visual Media. It considered the Media (as well as Hollywood) to be too much "under the influence" of the Left-leaning-intelligentsia. The members wanted "The Society" to become a pedagogic tool to interpret, in modern terms, the fundamental principles of what a true "free, economic society" should be, as expressed by classical Western economists (mostly British or belonging to the "Anglo-Saxon empirical/pragmatic/utilitarian school of the post-Enlightenment period"), political scientists, and philosophers.

Its work paralleled the work of another "society," i.e. The Atlas Network, created by the British national Antony Fisher in 1981. Fisher was directly influenced by the Austrian economist Friedrich Hayek's theories, who was then teaching (1945) at the London School of Economics. Having read Hayek's book *Road to Serfdom*, Fisher went to see Hayek and talked about his political desires to become an anti-Labor, anti-government, anti-regulations politician (what today in America is called an "anti-statist"). Smartly enough, Hayek convinced him that think-tanks were the best medium for promoting political change. The Mont Pelerin Society, therefore, kept close links with the Atlas think-tank. Formerly known as the Atlas Economic Research Foundation, Atlas was a nonprofit organization based in the United States. It took its name from Ayn Rand's Objectivist's magnum opus novel, *Atlas Shrugged* (1957). The novel's plot focuses on a dystopian United States in which the world of private business and entrepreneurship are thwarted under a heap of bureaucratic laws, regulations and governmental coercion. Railroad executive Dagny Taggart and her lover, the steel magnate Hank Rearden, struggle against "looters" and 'free-loaders" who want to exploit their productivity. In the meantime the dystopian society is afflicted by a "strike" of productive individuals who have retreated in a private Colorado's Shangri-La. The novel ends with the collapse of the "socialist" government, which allows "the strikers" to build a new society based on harmonious blend of reason, capitalism, and individualism.

It would be an easy guess to bet that Donald Trump read Ayn Rand's influential novel.

The Foundation's aims were, of course, to promote "free-market economic policies" across the world. The stated mission of the Atlas Network was to strengthen worldwide (forecasting already what will become the postmodern globalization of the economy) the "free movements" of capital, goods, and people by identifying, training, and supporting individuals with the potential to found and develop effective, aggressive organizations promoting capitalism and independent from any obligations, or duties of obedience. The Atlas Network was awarded many grants by corporations. One can wisely surmise that the CIA helped fund many of these propaganda (or counter-propaganda as they saw it) societies.

The movement gained momentum with the Neo-Conservative movement and the cynical, individualist materialism of the 1980s that seemed to have gained an ideological domination, especially in a culture which tends to believe that there is no underlying class warfare in its society. This is why, for instance, a professor from the University of Montana claimed, in the 1990s, to "have demonstrated" that there were no class-struggles in Butte (Montana), only ethnic conflicts!

The Neo-Cons figureheads, were, of course the British Prime Minister Margret Thatcher, and then, the Hollywood actor Ronald Reagan. The thinking heads were Ayn Randt with her metaphysical "Russian-obviated-mystical-individualism," and Milton Friedman's bullish capitalist ideology followed by his "Chicago Boys" (whose policies and influence were instrumental in the quick collapse of the Russian economy after the implosion of the USSR—something the Chinese government was smart enough to avoid).Their banking heads were the Koch Brothers, and the Scaife Family Charitable Trusts. Their propagandist and "advocatist" institutes were, and still are, the Libertarian Institute, the Reason Foundation, the Cato Institute, the Heritage Foundation, the

George Mason University's "Center for The Study of Public Choice." They are all institutions typical of the Republican "anti-statist" ideology. They all represent what has been called "Beltway economics", a diffuse political movement opposed to the down-town Washington liberal elites' control of the capitalist economy, considered to be mortally "statist" (something well illustrated by the HBO series *Billions*). To these institutions must be added the more or less secretive and manipulative lobbyist groups called the American Legislative Exchange Council, as well as the Americans for Prosperity, and The Generation Opportunity groups (all funded by the Koch corporation).

They all had had a strong influence on the Tea Party movement, and the Republican Party Freedom Caucus. In fact, Donald Trump fits to a T what these group stand for, except for his manipulative and demagoguic drift towards the people. President Trump is a *Mr Smith goes to Washington* gone "red-neck banker." A high-rolling, casino-real estate mogul who went "rightist populist;" a scion of the alliance between libertarianism (mixing up in a strange brew "free-market" ideology, concepts of metaphysical freedom, the " America is a land of opportunity" slogan, with a concept of "free society") and the politics of the wealthy elite.

Today, equality is receding far into the rear-view mirror of the accelerating drive of capital. Even during the Gilded Age and the Robber Barons period, when a similar ideology of economic elitism, Social-Darwinism, inequality and unfettered capitalist development reigned supreme, the socio-politics of the time succeeded in modifying, somehow, America's vastly unequal distribution of income and wealth over the course of a generation. It ended up fashioning a much more equal America, for a time.

Today, things are different.

The Keynesian trickling-down economic theory and praxis (favorable to governmental socio-economical regulations) has been replaced by a gushing-upwards-from-the-bottom financial flux, unbalancing the general economy. Over the last 20 years, an incredibly disproportionate share of America's income and wealth (caused by production gains and financial speculation) has flowed to the top of the nation's economic spectrum, causing society to be more and more governed by a limited "special class" ("in-corporation limited") of immense privilege and status, an oligarchy made up of mega-rich individuals and families. They are becoming the country's "hereditary aristocracy of wealth and power," while, at the other end of the economic spectrum, the majority of Americans' wages and savings dwindles. This situation is the result of policies and a politics which is nothing short of an unrelenting war waged against the bottom half of the population, aiming at the jugular of the life-support system of the nation and its people targeting affordable health-care insurance for the masses, Medicare, basic social government services, education… Instead are enacted taxation reforms benefiting the upper-crust, tax laws benefiting corporations supposed to increase investment…, reforms allowing a certain privatization of education (voucher system), as well as the privatizing of a maximum of governmental social services. All these measures are increasing the flow and fluxes of capital to the top of the social pyramid by lifting up all restraints. All these measures favoring the wealthy elite. This corresponds to a flight of an ultra-mobile capital levitating all certainties, assurances, issuances, vaporizing the object/subject oppositions, as well as metamorphizing the affective dimensions of human sociality and individuality. Whatever doesn't signify for the System, whatever is bad for its functioning, whatever it cannot absorb, whatever threatens to put the System in flight…, is itself put into flight. Everything that is bad within the system is loaded "onto the (scape-) goat of some sort" (scapegoat is *el azel* in Hebrew) and sent fleeing into the desert…, of obsolescence, irrelevancy, anachronic dysfunctionality, passéism—what the international critic Slavoj Zizek calls the "*Desert of the Real*." Is this what the ranchers and farmers of the so-called "Sagebrush Rebellion" feel deep inside while pointing an irate finger to "The Feds"? Contrary to what certain neo-Hegelians assert, capitalism does not really absorb and re-arrange all the negativity it produces. What it cannot deal with is merely sent flying away in the mirror of lost hopes. This is what, ironically, without knowing it, unwittingly, under the pretext of re-centering American politics on "the people," Trump is trying to do, like a capricious little boy in toy-store; that is, to throw everything "into flight" in the rear-view mirror of what is the past for an eternal present going at a futuristic speed.

Although there is a certain historical irony here, we do not know yet if the joke is on him or on us, or on us all.

Postmodern capital's speed and immateriality de-materializes everything: "*all that is solid melts into air.*"[29] These are visionary words since, not only is capitalism constantly expanding by con-quering new territories, creating new markets, pushing the limits of all horizons, and constantly revolutionizing itself in order to escape its own contradictions, but it leaves no stone unturned, nothing solid or permanent in its wake. It both destroys and conjures up into existence everything from cities to new configurations of production and "social-groupings." Moreover, the laws of exchange-value, linked to the primary one of sur-plus-value, the logic of circular permutation of all commodities and objects according to the values dictated by the same standard of equivalency, and the logic of commodity-fetishism, cause capitalism to reduce everything to a shadowy abstraction, a circulation of signs governed by the transcendental signifier known as money. The flow of the current or stream of exchange is governed by currency. The last 40 years of High-Tech hyper-development have accelerated the process to such a degree (what Paul

Virilio calls the determinative influence of speed on societies and human reality) that existence itself tends to become an illusion; a "reality" that the Wachovsky Brothers iconized by putting the novel onto the screen (*The Matrix*—1999).

Marx's prophecy is as prescient as ever.

In short, a whole host of phenomena, ranging from the porosity of national borders, de-territorialization (implying even the erasure of national borders), the actual and potential "globalization of contingency" in the form of global pandemics, ultra-violent tempests, sudden fluxes of emigration, and the specter of environmental catastrophe, to the backlash of increasing re-territorialization as new forms of paranoid sovereignty, renewed militarized forms of imperialism, international isolationism, political and religious fundamentalisms of all kinds, ethno-nationalist particularisms or irredentism, such as the projects for a "fortress Europe," or "making America great again"… , they all constitute reactionary trends and counter-pushes to stop the drift of reality (the change of space-time's coordinates), to counter-act (often unknowingly—and this is part of the problem) the radical/revolutionary thrust of postmodern, global capital.

Perhaps, it is now time to dwell on some numbers since, when one speaks about President Trump, one speaks about wealth, and phenomenal wealth. Let us start with four inter-related statistical figures.

Today in the U.S., according to the Institute for Policy Studies (*Billionaire Bonanza 2017*), the three richest men (C.E.O.s) in America own more wealth than the bottom half of the country. Employers make 300 times as much as workers, while half of high-schoolers come from low-income families and receive free or low-price high-school lunch; and only around 7% of private sector workers are unionized. Today, the wealthiest 25 individuals in the United States hold more wealth than the bottom 56% of the U.S. population combined, or 178 million people. In the US, according to *Forbes*, the 400 richest people who sit at the top of society own more wealth ($2.70 trillion) than the bottom 64% of the population. This sum is superior to the GDP of Great-Britain—the world 5th largest economy. In the meantime, 1 in 5 American households have a zero or negative net worth. All things considered, the bottom 1% of American households have a combined negative net worth of $196 billion, that is to say they owe more than they own. Of course, 30% of black households and 27% of Latino households have also zero or negative wealth, while the top 1% of the population have a positive net worth of $33.5 trillion. In 2012, more than half of all income went to the richest 10% of the population. These numbers have increased since 2012, re-enforcing the trends and widening the have/have-not abyss. All these figures put into perspective the reasons why and how the rich are getting richer, and the poor getting poorer (decade after decade), since the beginning of the "Ultra-Right reconquest" of the American socio-economic-political scene.

So why is the Trump electorate so blind or deaf? Why are they the willing instrument of his *jouissance*, which implies excess, posturing and imposturing?

Is it because, as the writer E.M. Cioran puts it in *A Short History of Decay*, "*there is a* plenitude of decline *in every overripe civilization*"? Because "*Instincts slacken; pleasures dilate and no longer correspond to their biological function; the voluptuous becomes an end in itself, its prolongation an art, the avoidance of orgasm a technique, sexuality a science. Methods and literary inspirations to multiply the channels of desire, the imagination tormented in order to diversify the preliminaries of release, the mind itself involved in a realm alien to its nature and over which it should have no purchase—all so many symptoms of the impoverishment of the blood and the morbid intellectualization of the flesh. Love conceived as a ritual makes the intelligence sovereign in the empire of stupidity. Our automatisms suffer for it; shackled, they lose that impatience to let loose an inadmissible contortion; the nerves become the theater of lucid discomforts and shudders, sensation in short extends beyond its crude duration thanks to the skill of two torturers of studied voluptuousness.*"?[30]

Trump wants to persuade Americans that capitalism can work for the people, instead of the people working for capitalism—although this is a moot point, since it is inherent to the political system itself.

In order to achieve this work of prestidigitation, Donald Trump has to make a heavy use of the Media, to trump the Media into playing his hand, and not theirs.

Ronald Regan was the first President to blur the distinction between the Media, entertainment, and politics. It took a Hollywood actor (ironically, at one point in time, a President of the Screen Actors Guild founded in the 1930s) to push the reactionary and reformist Republican agenda onto the American people. He was the first to use the slogan "Make American great again." He was as vague, vacuous, empty, and incompetent as Trump, although he had a Hollywood stamina, self-assurance, and sophistication that Trump does not possess. Regan dominated the podium and the screen while Donald Trump's political behavior on the screen is mere posturing, oafish, and gaudy, although pathologically obsessed with the Media.[31] The closing of the public imagination in the West, the resurgence of populism and irrenditism go hand in hand with the Mediatic representation of political leadership.

Donald Trump adds a new twist to this representational scene of simulation and dramatization: the art of populist exaggeration and simulated pugilism.

Trump and Hulk Hogan[32]

Donald Trump's strategy is opportunistic and he knows how to tap into the logic of populist resentment, using its negative icons: the devalued good and the glorified "bad"; the subverting socialist and the ghastly terrorist, the defamed (heroic) policeman, "self-defeating Big Government," "perverse Washington," the loser, the illegal immigrant, the Chinese businessmen or Mexican traffickers. Many among them are perceived as stealing American *jouissance* from their rightful owners. All are figures of speech, so to speak, straight out of an all-star wrestling spectacle, where emotions, the struggle between the good, the bad, and the ugly, orchestrated by a basic viriloid, macho posture, dictate the rules of the game—a game reminiscent of the semiotics of Roland Barthes's *Mythologies*, as Judd Legum argues.[33] He correctly compares the contemporary form taken by our political scene (already described in the 1980s by the situationist Guy Debord as "*the society of the spectacle*") to the stage of an All Star Wrestling performance and competition.[34] The presidential campaign debates, the Media discourses of the different candidates, their Media screen actualization and rendition, take on the form of an open-air spectacle (the audio-visual Media speak about the "airing" of political discourses—"on the air" or "live"), where each candidate is under the limelight, or under a

direct light which leaves no shadows (like fighters
on a stage), generating an emotion without reserve
among the participants and the spectators. That is
to say that the political has now turn into a spectacle of increasing excess where the stage, the stakes,
tactical "trash-talking," and the content's formal
delivery, are constantly upgraded in order to retain
the attention and interest of the spectators:

> "*What the public wants is the image of passion,
> not passion itself. There is no more a problem
> of truth in wrestling than in the theatre. In
> both, what is expected is the intelligible repre-
> sentation of moral situations which are usually
> private.*"

Donald Trump has become a master-fighter or
prize-wrestler in the art of the emptying out of
interiority to the benefit of exteriority—i.e. the
outside signs of a more and more problematic
interiority.

"*The public is completely uninterested in knowing
whether the contest is rigged or not, and rightly so; it
abandons itself to the primary virtue of the spectacle,
which is to abolish all motives and all consequences:
what matters is not what it thinks but what it sees.*"[35]

There is no presentation here but mere re-presentation, or the mere "*presencing* of an absence," as the
French deconstructionist Jacques Derrida would
say. This explains the repetitive writing (as if afraid
of revealing a void and conjuring up an absence)
of the emotive/descriptive dimension of Trump's

speeches. Hence his famous pouts, scornful facial expressions, the despondent casting-down of his eyes, his disdainful gazes, his "head up" movements or head shakes, his sneers, chuckles, laughter, his body movements and impatient gestures—the semiotic "body-emoticons" of an infantile and spontaneous behavior worthy of a teenager in a schoolyard. They express the exhaustion of the content by the form in our post-postmodern world, as if we had too many forms and not enough content. More worrying is the fact that, like its "wrestling counterpart," this form of political spectacle, which stages a battle between good and evil (evil is a word Trump constantly repeats) is based on the assumption there is an immanent (or populist) form of justice, where the ends justify the means:

> "*The crowd is jubilant at seeing the rules broken for the sake of a deserved punishment. Wrestlers know very well how to play up to the capacity for indignation of the public by presenting the very limit of the concept of Justice, this outermost zone of confrontation where it is enough to infringe the rules a little more to open the gates of a world without restraints… Justice is therefore the embodiment of a possible transgression.*"[36]

Donald Trump unveils the form of a Justice which is, at last, made simple and intelligible in a world of arcane complexity and stupefying contradictions—and "*there's the rub.*"[37]

Trump knows how to appeal to the collective unconscious of "our lost souls," re-awakening the Western, negative registry of their repertoire, whose iconic fears and hatreds he knows how to use but not control—which may pose serious problems during his Presidency. This explains the sudden resurgence of hate speech, mail and email, graffiti, physical attacks…, etc., all the traditional purveyors of hatred and fear of the other (anti-Semitism, hatred of Arabs, Muslims, Blacks…). Even Aryans, Neo-Nazi groups, White Supremacists, Skinheads, and Klanswo/men feel that they have to amplify the song of "Trump the Siren." He may have let the genie out of the bottle but his East European, or Latino butler lost the cork, and his advisers are no big help.

The Savoir-Faire of the *Political Savior*

Moved by a Walt Disney and reality show understanding of life, and a far-reaching populist emotionalism, our "disenfranchised individuals" want a
system of political revenge. Of course, an ambient
and rampant Political Correctness has exacerbated
their anger by inflaming their frustrations, especially today when electorates' moods are so volatile,
irritable, and unpredictable. This is why they like
Donald Trump, who cruelly and crudely laughs at
everybody—the rich and powerful included. His
messages have the same vacuity, vagueness, sensa-
tionalism, and density as commercial messages or
TV ads. This re-assures and comforts them. They
are not alone; someone understands them.

In fact, Donald Trump is "the one" who brings
the interests of the individual (what s/he wants,
knows, fears…) to self-consciousness. Trump is
not a passive conduit expressing the desires of the
masses. He plays an active role in verbalizing these
desires and interests. He unveils/reveals them to
their owners; as Hegel would say, he accomplishes
the transformation of the individual's interests,
making them pass from an "In-itself" into a
"For-itself." He is the medium, the enabler of the
recognition by the individual of his/her own, best
(or worst?) interests. It is as if the affected individual was telling him/herself, "where there was just
an emotional mess and extreme anger, I now have a

sense of myself and of my world." It is through him that individuals become clearly aware of what they really want. Trump helps them concretize these interests and subconscious desires into political expressions, tapping into their hidden (half-said, half-muted) prejudices, beliefs and convictions. He is a master manipulator of class-identity.

If one resorts to a Freudian psychoanalytic point-of-view, or, even a Jungian one, one could venture to say that a complex back-and forth movement of introjection (which implies a process of assimilation) and not projection (which involves dissimilation) occurs between Donald Trump and his base. This psychoanalytic process explains the transference of libidinal and aggressive cathexis from an object in the environment of a Trump follower to the mental/psychic picture of that object in his/her affective mind —as, for instance, the transformation of illegal/undocumented immigrants into the repulsive, delinquent, rapist aliens "sucking the blood" of the nation.

A more post-Freudian or Lacanian point-of-view would allow us to say that the Donald Trump follower/individual/disciple incorporates into his/her super-ego the image of "the Master" (as "the subject" supposed to know—i.e. Trump's quasi-charismatic image of "Fair Savior" turns into political "Savoir-Faire"). This process makes the super-ego of the follower, or subject under the influence, "super-egoic." It facilitates the flow of intense libidinal impulses (or drives) from the "id" and the unconscious of the individual into his/her ego via the introjected image-object of Trump. The "disciple's" super-ego, his/her ego, and the image of the "political Savior" as introjected/assimilated image-object, all form a "super-charged, excited whole" or "libidinal continuum." In this scenario, the obscene behavior of "Young Trump" (i.e. when he was just a "play-boy/real-estate developer/investor mixture," long before he decided to become a Presidential candidate) can only increase the level of mass-libidinal-excitement ("What a man!" "He dares to say the truth!" "Nothing stops him!" "He calls a spade a spade!" "He tells it like it is!"…). This particular psychic/mental process explains the extreme oral enjoyment shared by the participants at a Trump Rally, as well as the pleasure expressed by Donald Trump himself. This also explains the discursive "ejaculations" of repressed affects peppering Trump's political speeches: sexual jokes and allusions, sexist and derogatory comments, viriloid displays, profanities, humiliating comparisons, insults ("Crooked Hillary," "Weak and Feeble Jeb…") and rude criticisms. Trump brings out the forbidden of Political Correctness, as well expressions of a juvenile bathroom humor (and the enjoyment of what Freud called the "polymorphous perverse" typical of the pre-Oedipal phase of infantile development). During his rallies, libidinal energy comes out, raw, crude, unmediated, spontaneous, uncensored, and unrepressed—like the "free utterance" of a child's "free play." His posturing and impostures, his "self-referential aggrandizing" and "self-idolizing ideations," at once products of two psychic registers (the "ego-ideal" and the "ideal-ego"), constantly fire right and left, like a 4th of July patriotic display. He publically uses his "ego ideal" as his political guide. This mania becomes an obsession that he asks the crowd to confirm again, and again, and again, as if he wanted his followers to help him recover a phantasmatic, infantile, narcissistic perfection that he projects on his entourage and especially his family and children. Donald, his "people," his entourage, his family…, all become entangled in the webs of an idealized "mutual admiration society." They are all "great people," doing "an amazing job." The grandiloquent munificence of his superlatives fit the expedite nastiness of his expletives. Trump becomes the leader of a "group ideal" (in many ways similar to a "gang of inner city-youths") united by common likes and dislikes, "*lieux communs*" and clichés—the "transcendental vulgarizations" of commoners. The psychoanalyst Janine Chasseguet-Smirgel explains in *Perversion, Idealization and Subimation*, that the figure of perversion and imposture is the expression of an internal adolescence that asserts itself as pregenital, i.e. the "famous," Freudian, polymorphous perversity.[38] When meeting Donald Trump, we constantly run into a gifted "problem-child."

This unfettered libidinal energy also explains the extreme expression of political anger, and xenophobic and racist excitement displayed by Trump's supporters during the Campaign. The *jouissance* of speech is given free reign. The more it lashes out during political rallies, the more pleasure accrues in the audience. Paradoxically and uncannily, willingly or unwittingly, Donald Trump immerses himself, via his speech, reflections, spontaneous reactions, and mannerisms, in what the French deconstructionist Jacques Derrida calls the "obscene supplement of the law;" obscenity being, at once, the obstacle to, and the condition of possibility of the political dimension. It is the obscene supplement of power, as well as its symptom. Of course, this obscene sexualization of the staging of political power, only exacerbates the Sado-Masochist ambiguity of the relation between the one who exerts power and the one subjected to this power. Donald Trump is a Sado-Masochist figure and manipulator. His "mass political theatrics" are akin to the "puppet-show" of Plato's Cave puppeteers. These "entertainers" walk back and forth on a parapet situated between the light of a great fire burning at the entrance of the Cave, and the prisoners chained in such a way that they cannot turn their heads towards the entrance of the Cave. While walking behind the prisoners' backs, the puppeteers handle and manipulate objects from the outside world (the outside of the Cave the prisoners have never seen or even glimpsed at) in such a way as to cast shadows on the wall the prisoners, mesmerized, are forced to watch.

But something more is at work in this postmodern form of populist, essentialist enjoyment.

As we know, racism is a form of "naturalization," or "essentialization," of what is perceived by a subject as an "intolerable, threatening otherness," which then takes on the life of an ideological, social (and anti-social) narrative. It is the by-product of an intensification of nationalism and jingoism. Both the intra-subjective and intersubjective, intrapersonal and interpersonal dimensions feed and re-enforce each other. Racism is based on a rejection by the subject, or "I," of a "threatening object," or disgusting "other," opposed to the "I." This undefinable, fuzzy, "weird and uncanny object," through primary and secondary identification processes, becomes tainted by abjection and is "metonymically naturalized" by consciousness (Jews, because they are Jews, like money—it is in their genes; blacks, because they come from Africa are closer to nature and animals…). Abjection is the subconscious manifestation, the "*twisted braid of affects and thoughts*" of "incestuous leftovers."[39] It is the indirect "re-presentation," and expulsion from consciousness, of the by-products of the incest taboo enforced by the paternal injunction and the super-egoic law. Periodically, throughout the history of societies, this "tainted objectless-ness" spills over into otherness in dramatic fashion, irrationally, without rhyme nor reason, and is projected onto strangers, foreigners, invaders, outsiders, immigrants, i.e. all those one considers to be intruding into one's domain of *jouissance*— which is the enjoyment of the subject. Abjection haunts the zone of contact between consciousness and the unconscious, the inside (what "I" let in) and the outside (what "I" do not let in; what "I" proscribe). But in order to better understand the ravages a badly contained (or ritualized…, evacuated) sense of abjection can produce in a society, one has to take a short detour and use the concept of "homogeneity," a precarious form at the mercy of violence, internal dissent, and contradictions in the system of production. This concept was first used in a seminal way by George Bataille, the 1930s Collège de Sociologie's main researcher, who made it, together with its antonym "heterogeneity," the key factor in his *Psychological Structures of Fascism*.

Generally subjects expressing an obsession (disgust and/or fascination) with orifices and menstrual blood (heterogeneous objects or signifiers) betray a symptomatic liminal over-presence of abjection, something Donald Trump clearly revealed when he told CNNs' anchor Don Lemon about his feud with Mcgyn Kelly who was quizzing him about his past, misogynistic comments during the August 8 2015 Presidential Debate:

> *"You could see there was blood coming out of her eyes… Blood coming out of her wherever."*

Both concepts give us the key, and important clues, to the gateway leading to a better explanation of the phenomenon of "fascistoid" or postmodern populisms.

"Homo-geneity signifies here the commensurability of elements and the awareness of this

commensurability: human relations are sustained by a reduction to fixed rules based on the consciousness of the possible identity of delineable persons and situations; in principle, all violence is excluded from this course of existence.

Production is the basis of social homogeneity. Homogeneous society is productive society, namely useful society. Every useless element is ex-cluded, not from all of society, but from its homogeneous part. In this part, each element must be useful to another without the homogeneous activity ever being able to attain the form of activity valid in itself....

Social homogeneity fundamentally depends upon the homogeneity (in the general sense of the word) of the productive system. Every contradiction arising from the development of economic life thus entails a tendential dissociation of homogeneous social existence. This tendency towards dissociation exerts itself in the most complex manner, on all levels and in every direction. But it only reaches acute and dangerous forms to the extent that an appreciable segment of the mass of homogeneous individuals ceases to have an interest in the conservation of the existing form of homogeneity (not because it is homogeneous, but on the contrary, because it is in the process of losing that character). This fraction of society then spontaneously affiliates itself with the previously constituted heterogeneous forces and becomes indistinguishable from them....

The very term heterogeneous indicates that

it concerns elements which are impossible to assimilate...

The heterogeneous world includes everything resulting from unproductive expenditure... [such as]... the waste products of the human body and certain analogous matter (trash, vermin, etc.); the parts of the body; persons, words, or acts having a suggestive erotic value; the various unconscious processes such as dreams or neuroses; the numerous elements or social forms that homogeneous society is powerless to assimilate: mobs, the warrior, aristocratic and impoverished classes, different types of violent individuals or at least those who refuse the rule (madmen, leaders, poets, etc.)."[40]

So the changing inter-relationships between homogeneity and heterogeneity, production and surplus/waste or uselessness redefine identity and subjectivity. The treatment/status of heterogeneity, linked to abjection, by homogeneity define/re-define posture and erection (mastery/standing-up) of the citizen-subject. What is uneasily "put to rest" at the borders of bodily integrity and subjectivity to help us re/assure our limits by delineating an outside from an inside, by designating an "otherness" from a "selfness," is always in a state of effervescence. What is rejected by the subject's identity and selfhood for protection, has the tendency to come back to negatively haunt the subject/citizen/national—like the unconscious, which, by the way, for Bataille, is contained in the heterogeneous dimension. Consciousness and the unconscious, liminality and sub-liminality, frontiers and borders, nomads and immigrants, the stress, tensions and contradictions brought about by a global, ultra-capitalist production…, all are engaged in a very complex, chaotic and arcane bizarre dance; and all play a fundamental role in postmodern populism. This is why these effects and affects moving the postmodern subject also extend to what has been called the collective unconscious of a People, and the status of the Nation-State's identity and protection.

Donald Trump is at "the crux of the matter," i.e. a product of abjection and heterogeneity—in more ways than one. This sense of abjection speaks through his mouth, on and on. He is the motor-mouth, the porte-parole of the people's abjection: the abjection they feel about themselves, as well as the abjection they perceive at their borders threatening their life-style, values and 'jouissance": the heterogeneous other. What about Trump's own sense of abjection? As Bataille has shown us, paradoxically (or so it seems to us), the heterogeneous dimension encompasses in the same movement the inassimilable bottom of society (the dredges or lower-depths) and the summit of society (leader, tycoons, kings…). Likewise, for ancient Polynesians, the same taboo encircled what was at the top and at the bottom of their society: the gods and the filth.

The limits of subjectivity, selfhood and bodily integrity, become extrapolated and made to correspond to the strictures of citizenship, and to the borders of the Nation. Notions and concepts of safety/"threatening" immigration/Homeland Security then become paramount, especially in times of economic uncertainty, crisis or chaos. That is to say that periodically, in times of socio-economic duress, the rites, rituals and cultural practices which usually contain and control the abject, do not adequately accomplish their function. The abject is then left free to err like a floating signifier. It rapidly follows the "molecular lines" (Deleuze), fracturing the body-politic and the subjectivity of the citizen/consumer, attaching itself (tainting it) to the otherness which actually or not, in the imaginary or in reality, threatens the integrity/identity of the subject and the citizen.

"These body fluids, this defilement, this shit are what life withstands, hardly and with difficulty, on the part of death. There, I am at the border of my condition as a living being. My body extricates itself, as being alive, from that border. Such wastes drop so that I might live, until from loss to loss, nothing remains in me and my entire body falls beyond the limit—cadere, cadaver. If dung signifies the other side of the border, the place where I am not and which permits me to be, the corpse the most sickening of wastes, is a border that has encroached upon everything. It is no longer I who expel, "I" is expelled. The border has become an object. How can I be without border? That elsewhere that I imagine beyond the present, or that I hallucinate so that I might, in a present time,

speak to you, conceive of you—it is now here, jetted, abjected, into "my" world. Deprived of world, therefore, I fall in a faint. In that compelling, raw, insolent thing in the morgue's full sunlight in that thing that no longer matches and therefore no longer signifies anything, I behold the breaking down of a world that has erased its borders: fainting away... It is thus not lack of cleanliness or health that causes abjection but what disturbs identity, system, order. What does not respect orders, positions, rules. The in-between, the ambiguous, the composite. The traitor, the liar the criminal with a good conscience, the shameless rapist, the killer who claims he is a savior... He who denies morality is not abject; there can be grandeur in amorality and even in crime that flaunts its disrespect for the law—rebellious, liberating..."[41]

By negating/transgressing/erasing/denying borders and limits, the other expels the subject from its (Imaginary) center, its world. The border itself becomes not only objectified, it becomes "objected" and "abjected"; an object of worry for one's liminality, i.e. of anxiety about one's protective envelope and defense mechanisms. This explains the obsession of Donald Trump with the "Wall on the Southern border." In fact, in one of his (in)famous orations, Ui (the protagonist of Bertolt Brecht's *The Resistible Rise of Arturo Ui: a parable play*, 1941—a fictional 1930s Chicago mobster, who ends up controlling the cauliflower racket by ruthlessly disposing of the opposition), speaks about rapist immigrants who need to be kept out by a wall. This is familiar "Trump talk" and could come verbatim from one of his 2016 Presidential Campaign stump speeches. Trump willingly or unwittingly, summons in peoples' psyches affects and thoughts about the presence/absence of a "key object," a communal object or quasi-archetype, perceived by the subject as tainted and opposed to its self/ego, and therefore radically excluded from the subject's psyche for fear of drowning into meaninglessness and violent collapse. An illustration of such a fall of the subject into the abyss of nothingness is offered by Jordan Peele's directorial debut about paranoia and "zombie-ism" (*Get Out*, 2017) in postmodern societies, when the over-bearing coincidence of self/other in the subject is perceived as threatening to engulf the subject and annihilate its difference. Chris, the film's main Black protagonist falls into the "sunken place," after his hypnosis by the therapist-mother of his white girl-friend Rose Armitage. Another iconic treatment of such a symptom is offered by Hitchcock's film-noir/psychological thriller *Vertigo* (1968), when Detective John ("Scottie") Ferguson falls into a deep depression complete with catatonia, after his beloved Madeleine commits suicide by (seemingly) jumping from a bell-tower. Scottie's fall into the abyss of nothingness is hauntingly illustrated by the sequence of his body spiraling-down into a bottomless pit. In a way, postmodern subjects suffer from acrophobia and vertigo, which may explain why many regress into a frighteningly reactionary and essentialized stage of identity.

Muslim Fundamentalist terrorism as the ultimate "threatening otherness" has re-activated America's insecurities and fear of the "dangerous other," offering abjection new objects for investment. This explains the constant obsessional reference of Donald Trump to the "Wall" during the Campaign. The Master manipulates and embodies the fears and the collective unconscious of the People. His *I Will Make America Great Again*" is a slogan unknowingly for and against abjection. Its proscriptive prescription is tainted with the same ambiguity towards the border and the "abject other-object" as in Orson Welles' diegesis of *Touch of Evil* (1958). Trump's popular manipulations of the postmodern revival of a certain form of "populist abjection" in America, illustrate his own problematic, personal relation to abjection. Trump is the populist and popular revealer of people's political unconscious (Fredric Jameson's expression[42]) which makes him dangerous.

"The choice of my representative is not only my reflection-into-other, the mirroring of my interest in the political sphere, but simultaneously my self-reflection."[43]

Populism and Otherness

Disease and wellness, mass-psychogenic afflictions, and pandemics, reflect the anxieties of their time as well as the mode of consumption and the way of living, that is to say, the overall relation between the cultural sphere and the bio-sphere. To paraphrase Deleuze and Guattari, the social-libidinal investment of the "lost souls" revolves around a paranoiac, reactionary, "fascisizing" pole, as Susan Sontag explained in *Fascinating Fascism*.[44]

The political and emotional resurgence of populist nationalism in the West is predicated upon the irruption of a disturbing "otherness." The contemporary other (contrary to many other foreign "others" in the past) is now perceived as ultimately different, inassimilable, as if the body-politic of the nation could no longer ingest/digest the heterogeneous body of the "foreign other." Why is what used to be more or less accepted by Americans now unbearable?[45] Why does the "other" now hystericize Americans (and Western nationals for that matter) in a quasi-state of consensual hallucination—especially when they live in (relative) socio-economic affluence, relative to a majority of the world population? What has changed in the positioning of the subject with respect to others in the context of postmodern history and politics? Forgetting the exploration of the space of our solar system ushered by the promises of the Apollo Program, it is as if, for America and its satellites, immigration had become the final, socio-political frontier of globalization and its ultimate Imaginary investment.

Let us quickly indicate some reasons.

1. The child during the mirror-stage period (après Lacan) recognizes the image of something "other" as the objectification of itself and as him/herself in the mirror. This appropriation/re-cognition is based on a paradox: the coincidence of the self with an image of otherness is a construction which is the condition of the future differentiation between self and other, which is the basis of difference and identity (individual human/ the world), hence the triangulation between self, other and objects giving rise to the passage from cogito to consciousness. By the same token, meanings only emerge out of difference between words, in their in-between. This reverberates with questions of differentiation between ontology and the ontic, since for Heidegger, identity is caught in a hermeneutic circle. The ontological difference between "Being" and "being," circles back and forth between conditioning identity and conditioned identity. This explains the reversibility of identity and the tendency in humans to reduce the other to the identity of the body-subject. In order for difference to emerge there has to be a fundamental coincidence of self and other,

orchestrated by the *Big Other*. Although
unconscious, this structuring dimension is
linked to the *name-of-the-father* position.
One's identity can only be recovered as
difference, as Lacanian psychoanalysis has
shown. A characteristic of postmodern
capital is its subversion/erosion of any form
of regulation, constraint, temperance and
authority other than those it imposes. The
effects of this "grand deregulation" weaken
the *name-of-the-father* position, annihi-
lating its effects, increasing individuals'
difficulty in assuming or performing their
symbolic mandate; hence the postmodern
erring of our "lost souls," confusing intrasu-
bjectivitiy with intersubjectivity.

2. The identity-difference binary opposition lays the ground for objectivity. The
   Nation is the regulatory instance of the
   domestication of difference (self/other)
   and the condition for its transcendence:
   universalism. Universalism is being erased
   by postmodern capital, aggravating the
   affective positioning of the other in citizens'
   sense of national subjectivity. Since the
   history of race and the history of class in
   the US form a complex intertwined nexus,
   we should not be surprised to witness the
   (especially) white middle class's experience
   of loss of identity in racialized terms, which
   explains why many Americans are blaming

immigrants, Muslims, and people of color when they feel that their livelihoods are threatened. As we have seen earlier, the economic regional shifts triggered by neo-liberal globalization widen the "molar lines" (Deleuze) dividing and striating the social body, and especially those separating the urban and professional white "elite" from the increasingly precarious "non-elite." This exacerbation of tensions plays out as much through taste and cultural consumption as through economic anxiety, while increasing what Freud calls the "narcissism of small differences." This egotism then takes on a new life, blowing minute differences out of proportion, giving them a threatening dimension at the level of jouissance, as Slavoj Zizek explains very well in *Refugees, Terror and Other Troubles with the Neighbors: Against the Double Blackmail.*[46]

3. The neo-capitalist globalization has weakened the nation-state and the rule of law (the law representing/being, for Lacanians, the Other):

"The cause of this need for a violent imposition of the Law is that the very terrain covered by the Law is that of an even more fundamental violence, that of encountering a neighbor: far from brutally disturbing a preceding harmonious social interaction, the imposition of the Law endeavors to introduce

*a minimum of regulation onto a stressful
"impossible" relationship."*[47]

4. Transnational, corporate capitalism and
   consumerism, paradoxically, usher in a
   post-enlightenment period. The once stable
   boundaries between time and space, place
   and identity, human and machine, subjectivity and otherness, have become increasingly uncertain and in flux, bringing about
   an age of anxiety and making the once
   stable contours of life more elusive.

5. New Age ethical and narcissistic attitudes
   reduce the other (or neighbor) to one's
   mirror-image:

   *"to the means in the path of my self-realiza-
   tion (like the Jungian psychology in which
   other persons around me are ultimately
   reduced to the different discarded aspects of
   my personality."*[48] If this other disappoints,
   then via a boomerang effect, the self is
   destabilized.

6. Globalization, by making many laws irrelevant or obsolete, by eroding the governing
   instance of the Other, by cultivating the
   Imaginary (consumerism and individualism) radically upsets the fragile balance
   between identity and otherness.

For all these reasons, our "lost souls" and "com-
panions in disarray" feel that Donald Trump is the

guy they could have a beer with while cracking racist and sexist jokes to alleviate their sense of worthlessness, hopelessness and insignificance— projecting their self-deprecation onto "the other." Trump, whose "oral terrain" was well prepared during the last decade by speech and action-images such as stand-up comedians, crass Hollywood movies (*Meet the Fockers*—2004), reality shows, and extreme-rightist radio talk-shows, has erupted unannounced on the political scene, like a jack-in-the-box. It is the return of the "1950s' bad boy," complete and replete with the banana hair style, or "dick," raw and crude language, attitude, and displays of provoking vulgarity. Endowed with a peasant-like, or crafty businessman's common-sense, Trump wears his insensitivity (certainly the result of Sado-masochistic tendencies) like a "badge of honor."

Donald Trump overtly harbors the ostentatious mark of a projected "viriloid phallicism" (the "*toupé of toupet*") that he wears on his forehead, like the proboscis of certain monkeys. This over-determined, ostentatious, iconic presence of the masculine in Donald Trump, would direct us towards a certain feminine dimension of the character. His arborescent masculinity may function as a cache, something which will be explained.

But the joke is not only on him.

Trump and the Savoir of the *Postmodern Savior*

The joke maybe on the mainstream politicos and the Media pundits themselves:

> "*It is when the political powers think they have the masses where they want them that the masses impose their clandestine strategy of neutralization, of destabilization of a power that becomes paraplegic.*"[49]

Since religion and preachers are not what they used to be, sports, alcohol, guns (and not roses), are often the comfort of the new populist zealots of the besieged identities, while, deep inside, adding to their discomfort—something they would vehemently deny. They are rightfully scandalized by corruption, except that of their "Savior." But they do not know how to analyze its causes and draw the right conclusions, since public education has denied them the privilege to think critically and radically. This is why they are often clueless.

This "rightist exceptionalism" is not something entirely new in American politics. The rugged Arizona individualism and "Real Politik" of a Barry Goldwater, eons ago or so it seems, resonates with today's Tea Partiers and even Trumpists. Ross Perot, an ultra-utilitarian and pragmatic Independent presidential candidate, warned decades ago that free-trade agreements were not that free and that they would create a mass exodus of jobs from the US. But these rightist expressions never descended into the gutter. They always respected a certain consensus, while it now seems that political campaigning, public policy, leadership, respect and reason have descended in flames. It is as if the wrath of the multitudes polluted or wrecked the sanctimony of the official discourse of the High-er-Ups and experts.

The "disenfranchised folks" who voted for Trump feel that a rift is growing between their values and the reality of their daily lives; that the moral and legal norms are less and less part of their living experience; that the rug is being pulled from under their feet before they have had the time to say any-thing; that they are becoming irrelevant, obsolete; and this does not only affect "white men" as some "liberal" critics would conveniently like to think. Although voters in general mirror what is happen-ing around them, *"Terrorist strikes. Global shifts of power and influence. Bitter acrimonious partisan debates. And a fundamental question as to where traditional Western democracy fits in a new world order,"* most want "better"—not only just "change for change sake."[50] But instead of blaming the right culprit, i.e. postmodern capital and globalization, these new tea-partiers blame Washington, Big Government, and its past representative, Obama, whom they did not even honor with "President." They are not totally wrong, since, in Washington, around 50,000 lobbyists make sure that corporate interests, and those of the 1% upper-crust, are protected.

Without knowing it, they have the pathetic grandeur of *déclassé* social groups, of individuals who have lost a war—like the soldiers and steel-workers of Michel Cimino's *Deer Hunter* (1978).[51] This is perhaps why they like hearing that a Republican President will re-build the army and navy—as if "their" army had been destroyed.[52] But as we have seen, truth is of no importance, although, touchingly, they are looking for mysticism and lost meanings. But they are unwilling and unable to pay the financial price that their desire for regaining "lost grandeur" would entail (a "NASA Mars Program" similar to the "Apollo Moon program"—for instance). They also lack the basic education to imagine an alternative socio-political reality, or the "tools of the mind" (the intellectuality they despise so much), which could give them the weapons to forge a new destiny.

In a previous era, they would have become fascists—Nazis, brown, or black shirts.

Now they are mere products of a clash of ideologies caught in cultural wars whose meanings and control escape them.

Now they are just victims of the end of history, a post-history where everything becomes more and more hyper-virtual, meaningless and obfuscated. They are the victims of postmodern capital and globalization which de-territorializes everything (a Deleuzian term[53]), cultures and people included. They are victims unwilling to listen to other victims, whose plight is more serious than theirs—which precludes them from forming significant alliances or universalist coalitions—a phenomenon the System encourages and nurtures.

They are not people of the book (although they know The Book—or Bible) since they do not read any longer. The System would hate that anyway, and guards against it, by keeping them ignorant, favoring two-year and community colleges, where they learn a trade and the skills to make them good, efficient, and obedient workers. To keep them away from deep-reading and the critical scrutiny of politics, the System, via its High-Tech entrepreneurs (men who decide our future for us), favor the phasing-out of writing and reading printed texts. In a culture which cultivates the explosion of the Imaginary (Lacanian meaning), entertains the specific socio-cultural forms of desire which capture subjects' identification, and where misinformation and manipulation of facts and data is everywhere, their anger, supported by well-heeled interests, feels empowered by the daring master-lies of their "*porte-parole.*" In fact, the bolder the lie, the more believable it becomes. Their anti-intellectualism has become an anti-humanism (which they perceive to be "secular"—therefore nefarious) which has turned into an anti-humanitarianism and an anti-internationalism. In Montana, some of their representatives in Helena have voted for an "anti-sharia law," while some counties unanimously declare themselves "United Nations free-zones." They do not sport passports anyway. By the same token, they are suspicious of politeness and diplomacy. They perceive them as "phony" put-downs of their "crudeness" and spontaneity. They believe that their direct, unsophisticated manner of "speaking plainly" is indicative of their genuineness. There is a trace of class resentment in their attitude. This is why Trump, who masterfully splits the combined jurisdiction of politeness and politics, appeals to them. Consequently, they shun any culture which is not popular/populist—especially the "highbrow one." PBS is their enemy—the Cable Guy their idol. Consequently, they just surf the ocean of messages and information they do not wholly understand, unable to read the winds of geopolitics, to tell the South from the North, the East from the West. For them, deserts or forests are the same; they are accordingly hot or cold, drenched or dry, but always dangerous, foreign and malevolent places; only suburbs and malls are secure and homey. There is an immanent sadness in their refusal to believe in the reality of facts, in their desperate, dogged determination to negate the right conclusion. They are romantic (or "kitschy-romantic") without knowing it, something which comes out through the deep, moving, at times agonizing, pulses of country music. When the pressure builds up and becomes too much, they move to the "American wilderness," where they can hunt and fish in peace, that is without too much government intervention, in Idaho, Montana, Vermont, Wyoming, or Alaska, preparing for the Apocalypse, re-enacting the Western myth of the individual pulling himself up by his own bootstraps, playing "survivalists" ("preppers"). This is why many people at the "end of their tether," cut the "umbilical cord" and "go native." Militia men and women, fierce Independents, Cultists, and Extremists of all sorts "go off the grid" in the wilderness. For them, even a Donald Trump has no usefulness.

Basically they are good people—or see themselves as such. They are your neighbors, your parents, office employees, or distant cousins. They also live in each of us, a little bit, hidden—whether or not we want to admit it. The French call them "*beauf*."

They are human, inhumanly human—and the signs that our postmodern society is failing, and that there is neither democracy, nor transcendence of the object.

Donald Trump: Trump-Card or *Trompe-l'Oeil*?

As Nancy Isenberg recalls in *White Trash. The 400-Year Untold History of Class in America*, the postmodern, post-politics phenomenon we could call "Trumpism," is nothing really new in American politics with their quirky, democratic games. From the Andrew Jacksonian type of populism to James Vardaman, from William Randolph Hearst to Governor "Big Jim" Folson, with his bare-foot parading on the stage, from Ross Perot to Sarah Palin, populism and popular demagogues and manipulators have always made good bed-fellows. In America, as Mike Davis explains in *City of Quartz*, the façade of populism has always dissimulated the operations and manipulations of an ultra-elite power structure, which in the 1900s, in large cities, routinely used to buy elections in the name of popular anti-elitism.[54] Also, as the political and cultural analyst Slavoj Zizek writes *"The onset of the post-'68 hedonist permissiveness that was part of the prospect of integrating nations into larger communities held together by the global market did not give rise to universal tolerance but, on the contrary, triggered a new wave of racist segregation."*[55] This new form of postmodern, Western populism, was already heralded in the early 1990s by the Eastern European shift from communism to a Western-style type of consumer democracy which witnessed the irruption of until then repressed forms of ideological, collective enjoyment" "*the eruption of enjoyment in the form of the re-emergence of the aggressive nationalism and racism that accompany the disintegration of "actually existing socialism" in Eastern Europe.*"[56]

What is different in the politics of our new "Gilded Age" is its seeming indifference to language, as if neo-capitalism, with its infernal dance of signs, had worn out the referential dimension, to use a linguist's term, and severed the last tenuous bond between reality and words. It is not only a question of truth versus lie, since in order to lie, one has to believe that truth exists. It is more the reflection of a total indifference to truth. This indifference is the result of, and in turn produces, dis-information (the stuff advertising and propaganda are made of)—in a word, "bullshit;" the perfect formal receptacle for paranoia and popular anxieties. This oral, inchoate void constitutes a silent discourse in search of a Master-Signifier, or an instance or person who knows how to soothe and give a voice to the "savage breast" of the populace's fears for the future. Trump's discursive dimension displays the type of bad faith characteristic of pathological liars. He knowingly steers his discourse between trickery, ambiguity, and error. But his speeches would not convince his fans if they did not already expect them; if they were not already persuaded by them—as if pre-ordained by their own unconscious. Since humans' egos are subordinated to the law of recognition, Trump's followers are vulnerable to flattery. Hearing what they want to hear re-enforces their egos.

Trumpism as a right-wing, political populist movement is as vacuous as the architecture of its Master.[57] Like his buildings, copy-cats of other architects' buildings, generic towers free of any vision, Trump is a pure signifier, empty of any essence or content, filling up the signified with an ostentatious "expedient whatever"—anything that will help gain ascendance or the upper hand. His towers, monuments to himself, do not bear the stamp of any artistic innovation, except his passion for seeing his name plastered everywhere. In that sense, since the word postmodern was invented in relation to architecture, Trump is a pure postmodern phenomenon. His own, private, opulent Manhattan penthouse, on top of this own Tower, is full of rich and lavishly gaudy adornments, and iconic "*nouveaux riches*" displays, with gold accented furniture à la Louis XIV ("The Sun King"), as if to compensate for the vacuity of their design, and the rather "Moon-like face" of their Master-Proprietor. The Presidential Tower is a "kitschy-downtown-jewel-box" for his trophy wives.

As we have seen, in his discourses and speeches, the signified, playing the role of a pretext, or an additive, comes a-posteriori. This is perhaps why he emblazons his towers with a "double T" ("Trump Tower"). This redundancy iconizes the provoking pun, "*I am a monument*,"[58] a term coined by Robert

Venturi while arguing in favor of Las Vegas Strip's "ordinary and ugly" type of architecture (kitsch) against the qualities of "heroic" modernist architecture. Venturi seemingly ignores the fact that the monumentality of postmodern architecture, which hovers over the skyline as if aiming at privatizing the sky itself, also empties out the city of what is left of public spaces. In many ways, Donald Trumps' style and politics form an exemplary postmodernist text. Like Venturi's architecture, it is a call for pastiche as well as ironic provocation. They inscribe themselves in a dialectical tug-of-war between skepticism (doubt of the unknown) and the matter-of-fact mundane, expressive spontaneity (language of common, ordinary life) and the deadpan of the void, symptomatic ipseity and glib dismissal. Donald Trump's lifestyle and discourse and the quintessentially American city ("Sin City"), whose architecture Venturi celebrates, have one thing in common: they both appeal to the populace and the wealthy elite.

The New York Trump Tower which, at the time, was the first "super-luxury high-rise tower of mixed-use," is a monument devoid of any meaning, except the one assigned to architecture and city-planning by financial speculation. It represents a proliferation of signs exempt from any superior, transcendental meaning, except the ones that it gives to itself, in obedience to the laws of the market. Similarly, Venturi's architecture expresses the forms of late capitalism, where the metastasis of a complex aggregate of signs and signifiers (qua-si-orgiastic as in the case of Las Vegas) pre-empts or supplants the form-based meanings of modern architecture, as well as the sign/symbol-based meaning of postmodern architecture. Venturi's architecture is "neo—post-modern." If one wants to describe the Donald Trump phenomenon and politics more accurately, one would have to say that they already beyond the postmodern and are in-dicative of a neo-post-modern shift, although both Venturi and Trump obey the logic of postmodern capital, to borrow from Fredric Jameson.

"In Trump's case, the signifier, evacuated of all mean-ing, tells us precisely what the buildings are not. What they are, by most accounts, is empty—many of the apartments within have been snapped up not as homes but as investment properties for out-of-town-ers who rarely stay there."[59]

In the case of the Trump Tower, this ipseist, empty redundancy is the unconscious expression of a truncated self in need of lengthening and expansion, or the unconscious desire to indicate one's limitations, by barring the megalomaniac, hyperbolic form-based meaning of the "I," with the horizontal movement of erasure, of castration. It is perhaps both as the contradictory symbolic origin of the "T" seems to indicate—at once a symbol of guilt, shame and death, and a symbol of renascence, life and vitality. The cross is the sign of the crucifixion of the son in the name of the father.[60] As any good "savior," Donald Trump bears his cross, albeit golden, without knowing it. He is doing it for the people and for the "cause," throwing in his millions for it. But there is more to "it" than the cross can bear.

The contradictions of Donald Trumps' behavior are not conditioned by the objective contradictions of his own socio-economic and cultural situation (Sartre's favorite explanation while psychoanalyzing Gustave Flaubert's existence in the *Family's Idiot*—1981), but by his own internecine contradictions, i.e. his symptom—and Donald' s symptom speaks a lot.

"*I wrote The Art of the Deal. I say not in a Braggadocious way…*" announced Donald Trump when sparring with Hillary Clinton during the September 26 Presidential Candidate Debate.[61] Without going as far as saying that "*he doth protest too much…*,"classical etymology shows us that the word "braggadocio" is a signifier whose sound-image can be peeled back in layers.[x] Used, for instance, in the late Renaissance epic poem *The Fairie Queene*,[62] it possesses a complex etymology of Old Germanic, Celtic and Latin origins, as well as modern English and French usage. What is interesting and relevant in the case that concerns us, is that "braggadocio" antithetically mixes the "high-brow" with the "low-brow." It brings, in an oxymoronic fashion à la Lévi-Strauss, seeming opposites such as the face and the arse, since the Old Celt "brag" (English "breeches") connotes at once ostentatious clothes (French *braies*) and bombastic, superlative rhetoric; i.e. "bragging." But the alliteration does not stop there, because "brags" or "breeches" cover a certain part of the male anatomy. Brag/breeches conjure up "smug" and "mug," "rag" and "rogue," as well as "prig" and "prick"...[63] A "braggadocio" is someone who, therefore, wears his breeches on his head, unveiling it all, taking off the "cache" (and therefore any restraint/constraint) in order, perhaps, to convince us that he has "*it*."[64] A "braggadocio" connects levity with lewdness, exhibitionism with insecurity. Perhaps Trump's unconscious was telling us the truth of its master-discourse on that fateful evening which, by the way, was not that fateful. If, the day after, there was a dramatic drop in his ratings, Comey's announcement about the F.B.I. investigation of the Clinton Foundation changed everything and brought his ratings back up again, rendering him the "winner" of the debate.

Trump's dimension also conveys notions of human excess, the subject of famous artistic or literary clichés such as Shakespeare's Falstaff, many Balzacian characters, Orson wells' Citizen Kane, or, more ominously, Alfred Jarry's *Ubu Roi*, or even a Benito (Mussolini)—the king of "braggadocios." He comes off as an outrageous psychological machinery, in constant need of instant gratification (admiration, sex, food, energy…). It is a type of "gratification-need" a psychoanalyst would have a heyday analyzing. Donald constantly moves his lips, forming quasi-libidinal "Os," as if he had been weaned too early. Here ultra-labial-prehensility for the breast, and anxious apprehensiveness of the lack, reinforce each other. His strong oral drive manifests itself via lips pursing, smacking, pouting, puckering, a whole body semiotic of oral frustration and want of gratification. His hair, lips and mouth, dark-suit-covered belly, and the presence of an obsessional penis that he indirectly flaunts via his constant bragging and posturing of his (masculine) superiority (Lacanian phallic function) structurally function as the unconscious and Imaginary sites and icons of his persona. They have become his fetishes which paradoxically dramatize his magnificence and munificence ("I finance my own campaigning!"). Like a fetish, Donald Trump aspires to sacralization via power and popular adulation. He wants to be objected and cathected as such by his subjects. His constant, prolix, repetitive utterings, rambling and wavering, presidential ukases, diktats and counter-diktats, public notices, press communiques and daily "twitting twitters," his smiles and frowns…, are the primary signifiers of his official body—his body-politic. They also serve as objects of verbal and popular mockery. Usually these psychic constituents are the intrinsic, albeit erased or repressed elements of any official, political discourse. Rabelais, the great Renaissance writer, and the Russian critic Mikhail Bakhtin gave splendid illustrations (which still live in us) of the obscene, vulgar or grotesque elements located in popular, non-official or subversive cultures targeting the official discourse of power, such as the dramatized excesses of reversal of the Carnival.

Symptomatically enough, Donald Trump brought out the repressed dimension of politics and personal/private discourses to the forefront of the public arena. Is it the effect of an uncontrolled simulation of stereotypes? Is it the effect of an Imaginary self-reflection of power caught in the psychic primary dimension would a Lacanian say? Or the plebian by-product of a self-legitimating authoritarian personality short of transcendental materials? Whatever the cause, Trump came up trumps by playing the political buffoon, and using obscene and grotesque images and vocabulary which normally would have undermined any other official postulation to the Presidency, as if he was mocking the whole process itself. Traditionally the language of the body and the unconscious (the grotesque, the obscene, the vulgar and bawdy, the verbose earthiness…) is the most efficient way of deriding politics, deconstructing or de-legitimizing authority and power. But Trump's cosmically and cosmetically comic performance is not perceived as a negative by his electorate. Trump is a gushing mouth who seduces and colonizes the populace's Imaginary. The postmodern marriage between "pomp and circumstances," pomposity and mockery, banality and luxury have served him well.

As a self-appointed, although now by the masses anointed, "*Tribun du people*," a populist figurehead à la Danton, without the philosophy and sense of emancipatory history, Donald Trump is constantly motivated by a desire to fill up a huge "inner vacuum." For instance, he has such a need for gratifying attention and immediate results that, right after a political speech, like a child, he has to furiously consult the polls and tweet his followers to make sure that he is still loved, admired and followed. For this purpose, he uses his "non-secure cell-phone" that any serious hackers can access. Political analysts, when speaking about his "enormous ego," may not be on target here. Rather than a huge ego, Donald Trump seems to be characterized by a large lack—which explains the accumulative and superlative dimension of his "toys": huge towers, incessant speeches, heaps of money, beautiful women galore, large planes bearing his "coat-of-arms" (his name), crowd adulation…, a Versailles-like penthouse in his vertical donjon… The only gadget missing is a Trump-mobile. Donald does not wear his heart on his sleeve. He wears his lack on his head, like a clown, as a toupé…, or "braggadocio." He dares, defies and challenges us via his ostentatious, "testimonious" lack, his "show-and-tell" that he is not afraid to endorse and wear provocatively. The U.S. Presidency represents the ultimate adornment, the pinnacle of his career of accumulation and denial that he can erect on his own towering shoulders, so that he can stand on his own shoulders—a clone of himself, a tribute of himself to himself. The future will show if he knows how to turn his Rabelaisian dimension into a force to be reckoned with, and a politics for all to share; or if he fails miserably.

Trump pumps up the world and ideas of his peers politicos and financiers alike. He is as mimetic as a chameleon. We have to keep in mind that, although Trump only ran on the Republican ticket, he is no more Republican than he is Democrat. This is why a Trump speech can so easily turn upon itself, negating his previous utterances. But, like a high-wire walker, or a clever stage performer, he avoids (pit)falls; nothing fazes him. Backlash-effects are met with total denials. If hooked up to a generator, his back-pedaling could cover the electricity needs of a whole modern city for at least a night. Is he a "celibate machine," an "automaton on a mission," or "the bachelor who stripped the bride bare," à la Marcel Duchamp—which would cast a new light on his past "groping adventures"? He can rebrand himself and fit any sky, any climate—although he thrives under authoritarian clouds. This is perhaps why he likes Vladimir Putin so much; with him he seems to share affinities. But this is another story.[65] He has no strategy. He is mere tactics. At his stand, the performer must stay put, his head high, keeping up appearances. He only allows himself to pout rebukes away, like a little boy who was just denied a treat by Mommy.

Trump Capitalism or the Emptiness of his Populist Economics

Trump's *fuck-them-all* attitude, with its Giulian-iesque nastiness (or would it be Rumsfeldesque?), its quasi-Kardashian relentlessness and brazen, kitschy vulgarity, epitomizes the Zeitgeist of our modern neo-capitalist ethos. It appeals to our civilization of reality TV. It is *Duck Dynasty* goes to Washington. Nancy Isenberg explains in the chapter "*Outing Rednecks*" of her magisterial study about white trash and class in America, how the Trump phenomenon was prepared and ushered onto the political scene by a systematic Media hype about the life style of the very people Madison Avenue and Hollywood used to viciously lampoon and pitilessly mock; as if the upper-crust was hiding its "classist ideology" and "anti-working-class bias" behind a mockery of the American lumpen proletariat's oddity and weirdness—i.e. the poor Appalachian or Southern rural folks, the "white niggers" of the American South. This type of "wild exoticism" mixed with racist disgust used to be directed towards Afro-Americans or Hispanics, or towards the Irish—in Canada, the same type of racism used to be directed towards the rural Quebecois whom many Anglos used to call "*nègres blancs*" in the 40s and 50s. To which must be added the TV Reality shows and voyeuristic survival programs which glorify a suburban-type of "Darwinism

101," with its mock-pretense of "survival of the fittest" complete and replete with (chaste) primitive nudity and raw or ignoble food ingestion. Donald Trump does not know how to lie, because he is a "bullshit" master, and contrary to lying, "bullshitting" is indifferent to the truth. There is something disturbing and worrying behind this spontaneous, "no-holds-barred," gutsy, irrational form of populism; the perfect conduit for his tactlessness and personal vindictiveness. It is as if its "practitioners" or "followers," ("He's one of us") were, beyond their rejection of progressive politics, actually sick and tired of sex, of difference, of emancipation…, of culture itself. On the brink of an existential and emotional abyss, they seem to be only capable of looking back towards an (imaginary) original, organic togetherness; to the type of society which they think "had it together," when the black/brown were below them. Their nostalgia, propped up by a fear of the void, exacerbates their revisionist and reactionary political positioning, mixing up affects and emotions, cause and effect: *"The world of individuals and social relations itself offers striking examples of this exhaustion—or resistance—or nostalgic attachment to some prior state of being. In any case, we are dealing with a kind of revisionism, a crucial revision of the human race—a species unable to brave its own diversity, its own complexity, its own radical difference, its own alterity."*[66]

The same vacuity characterizes Donald Trump's theories about the economy. Buoyed by the

Republicans control of congress since 1994 (the first time since 1954), and the social, political and economic Neo-Con agenda of the Reagan era, Trump rides a wave already crested by Newt Gingrich (Georgia Republican Representative) with his "Contract with America," which ushered in the American Christian Right's nominal control of American politics.

His economics are not only old-fashioned, a re-hashing of recipes belonging to an older form of capitalism; they are also a pure semblance. If they work for the 1% at the top, i.e. the capitalists profiting from an unbridled system of financial speculation and manipulation of financial leverage, debts and futures, it is not possible that they will make a positive difference for the average daily working man and woman. They can only increase the militarization and capitalization of the System. His budget proposal, if it passes, will boost spending for the Defense Department (Veterans Care and Homeland Security included), while cutting the funding of all the others. Donald Trump's Cabinet boasts eight ex-executives from Goldman Sachs, the financial company famous for having "advised" the Greek government into bankruptcy, among many other speculative exploits. The President thinks that what is good for Wall Street is necessarily good for Main Street. He seems to have convinced his followers. For how long? Like Alfred Jarry's *pataphysics*, Trump's economic politics belong more to the "science of imaginary solutions" than to the harsh realities of today's political economy and the contradictory financial effects and economic contradictions of global capitalism.

The void of the signifier in Trump's world has leveled everything, giving everybody the impression that we are all equals—that we are all humans; that a poor sap could share a beer with a tycoon, or that a filthy rich playboy might deign to grab the crotch of a humble secretary.

What is more dangerous is that the *fuck-them-all* attitude turns into a *fuck-the-other* behavior, although his acceptance speech tried to soothe the bruises suffered by all during the most heinous and "un-personable" presidential campaign the country has ever known—it is now time "*for us to come together as one united people.*" But since Trump has said everything and its contrary, and has lied continuously, the future of his governance is highly problematic.

An insight into Trump's type of capitalism is offered by Brian Massumi in *Normality is the Degree Zero of Monstrosity:*[67]

> "*Neoconservatism is the clear perception by a liberal nation-state of the capitalist attractor in all its purity, as a virtual pole of existence. It is the coming out of capital, a new golden age of greed that dares to say its name. Without a wince. Capitalism no longer has to justify itself. It no longer has to hide behind fascist-para-noid quasicauses and argue that it serves the*

common good. It can dispense with belief and good sense, because it is now stronger than molarity, and stronger than the ideologies that help to reproduce it. The men who personify it—the Donald Trumps and Michael Milkens of the world—do not so much represent an ideological cause as embody a desire. An abstract desire, a mania for accumulating numerical quantities. Possessing things is understandable from the moral-molar point of view, as is wanting to accumulate capital for what it can buy in the way of time, things, and activities. But to accumulate more than anyone could ever spend? And then keep on accumulating greater and greater sums, with no other interest or aim in life? That is beyond good and evil. The neo-conservative capitalist is defined less by what he possesses than by what possesses him. He is the personification of a mode of irrationality. In itself, the agency of that irrationality is not abstract like the quantities it begets and induces these post-human bodies to accumulate. It is superabstract.[68]

Trumpism

To give Trump some credit, he knows his constituency and has consistently followed his intuition for the past two years. He realized that many Americans' anger and uncertainty in the face of the inexorable march of globalization and technology had reached such a level that voters were ready for disruption at any cost: Away with the elites! Enough of experts! The list goes on. Enough of status quo! Away with Political Correctness! Off with the liberal intelligentsia, cultural pundits, and incomprehensible artists with their predominant place in the media (they make us feel dumb and dumber)! Away with stagnant incomes and off-shored jobs! Away with Washington—which may partly explain the reluctance of Mrs. Trump to move to the White House!

Their message has become Trump's message. Although a New Yorker (who does not like Washington and its French layout—he prefers the Towers and Walls of The Big Apple into which he has bitten successfully over and over), he succeeded in manipulating and capitalizing on the frustrations of the Heartland so well (a remarkable sleight of hand in itself) that even the Democrats' strongholds of Michigan, Pennsylvania, and Wisconsin voted for Trump. He quickly realized that the American blue-collar workers, abandoned by both parties, were furious about the fact that the type of jobs which allowed them to buy a home, a car, and a college education for their children on a working-man's wage (the American Dream), disappeared or were replaced by lower paying jobs without benefits, and a credit-based consumerism. As these jobs moved to very low-salary "developing" countries, the blue-collar union workers (who were once the base of the Democratic party in the Northeast and Midwest) also lost their benefits and pensions, since service industry jobs cannot be compared to "unions jobs." Trump tapped into the deep and widespread pool of discontent–even if its waters were murky. NAFTA, the North American Free Trade Agreement initiated by President Clinton and voted for by Democrats and Republicans alike in the 1990s, wrecked havoc in the American manufacturing belt. Former good-paying manufacturing jobs throughout the Midwest left for non-union labor jobs South of the Border, transforming Mid-America into a huge Rust Belt, turning formerly prosperous middle-class and working-class communities into mere sad whispers of themselves, and once vibrant cities into economically war-torn wasteland (such as large swaths of Detroit).

The "builders of America" felt forgotten and put their bets on a "Savior" who would restore the American dream (hence the rallying-cry "Make America great again!"). They claim, or pretend to believe, that an unconventional, brazen business tycoon knows how to restore prosperity to the middle-class (since the expression "working-class" has now become a dirty word in America). Feeling abandoned by the "Clintonian Democrats," they became populists. Of course, talking the talk is not the same thing as walking the walk—which means that this electorate showed a certain amount of gullibility by putting their bets on an ultra-rich "banskter" (although Trump is no banker), the type who caters to the desires of the very rich, and who is certainly going to surround himself with Wall-Street's "*who's who*." But many Americans still believe in trickle-down economics. They became seduced by a demagogue's discourse which encouraged them to blame their socio-economic problems on immigrants (especially "the little brown people"), environmental regulations, unfair trading, and the decline of law and order. What they are not anticipating is that the effect of this new, post-Reaganesque deregulation will certainly roll back all the regulations and rules that keep our environment relatively healthy, and curtail or suppress the few social safety nets that still make people's lives tolerable.

Will the good-paying jobs and high-quality products be "in-sourced" (or "re-sourced") and come back to our shores, and will America become great again? This is doubtful since America's problems and anxieties are due to economic, structural problems, that is, the problems due to the contradictions inherent to global capitalism. A nationalist capitalist, Donald Trump is no Bernie Sanders. His extreme nationalism is even absurd and a testimony to his brash, gold-plated philistinism. By trade, conviction, and philosophy, he will never be able to implement policies which will directly tackle and counteract the contradictions of capitalism and its socio-economic impacts on the population. So whom will the people blame then and what will they do?

This victory over Hillary Clinton upset the American political establishment. The elites of the East and West coasts, in their smug arrogance, did not see it coming, with their dismissiveness and ignorance of the Heartland's anger and the "commoners' frustrations," which fed Trump's rise. Remember Reagan's praise for the "common man," or Bush's use of "Joe the plumber" during their election campaigns. Some analysts, and Trump himself, have compared Trump's populist success to an "American Brexit." It seems that the vaguely anti-globalist, nationalist, and xenophobic populist forces behind Britain's surprising and problematic exit-vote from the E.U. are similar to those which carried Trump to victory in America. The disenfranchised of Main Street, the "globalization's forgotten" or "marginalized" (interestingly enough, not the ghettos and inner-city paupers) often living lives of precariousness, arose and spoke. Hillary Clinton was never in tune with their frustrations as the popular success of Bernie Sanders showed. She used to mock, during her campaign, the vacuity of Trump's claim to "make America great again" by saying that "America is already great." In spite of her political savvy and experience, she never fully understood that America is not great for everybody. Clinton's sudden political retreat from the TPP (Trans-Pacific Partnership) only came as a late political maneuvering, when pressured by Sanders' supporters. Her opportunistic move did not convince the Rust Belt victims.

Trump's election was followed by demonstrations of angry young protesters in many American cities, voicing their anxieties and disappointment, and there was no overall celebration. What a difference from the victories of Barack Obama in 2008 and 2012, when cheering crowds of mixed classes, races, and ages, gathered in Times Square! The silence of New-York, the international megalopolis, a stronghold of the Democratic Party, was telling. Nobody seems to know what to make of the revenge of Middle America, above all of a (white) working-class America troubled by changing social and cultural mores.

Trump's election comes at an uncertain, agitated, and volatile period in world affairs. Although Trump has shown a "royal contempt" for many American values (respect for diversity, inclusiveness, separation of the judiciary and the executive…) and even mocked the democratic process itself, given the fact that American democratic institutions are strong, and that the United States has nothing in common with Weimar Germany, one should not be especially worried about his Presidency, and a possible drift towards a new form of fascism. With a Republican majority in the House and Senate, Trump will have enormous power, much more than President Obama, constantly confronted by a stubborn, partisan, Republican Congress. But, as we also know, the System frames the Presidency in such a way that its margins of action and maneuvering are very limited, and its powers are often purely symbolic, as President Obama bitterly experienced; or as President Kennedy's tragic end epitomizes, if one lends credence to conspiracy theories.

Trump is a businessman, ill-prepared for the Presidency, without any real political experience, beyond the one acquired during his drastic, vehement and redundant campaign, which has revealed personal flaws for all to see: impetuous anger, meanness, mendacity, whimsicality, superficiality, and petulance. His Cabinet's ability to control his diva-like outbursts will be of critical importance for the future.

It looks like we should have paid more attention to *The Simpsons* which, 27 years ago, forecast Trump's presidency. So the lesson learned from that is to watch more *Simpsons*, and also *Family Guy*. It did not have to be this way. But that is what happens when the plight of the working class is ignored for so long. When the Democrats support policies which ignore the negative impacts on the working-class; when the proverbial can keeps getting kicked down the proverbial road; when the so-called "party of the working class" has long since sold them out; when corruption and money oil the political machine from the top to the bottom…, and on, and on, and on. People lash out—very often irrationally. But they are fed up and with their backs against a wall. Let us hope that they did not wall themselves in, and in the process, all of us. The ultimate enigma is the role of the logic of neo-capitalism in the whole process. Besides the propaganda, which played a crucial role in eroding American consciousness, besides the law-and-order State, where the majority of citizens believe that liberty and equal rights for all are firmly entrenched legally and guaranteed by the constitution, who are the "string-pullers"? Whose is the tail which wags the dog? Who are the self-interested groups and individuals? Do they think they can manipulate the vast amount of followers the "charismatic maverick" has succeeded in gathering, as well as control, at the same time, the "fancy demagogue" himself, for their own gain?[69]

The United States of Trump

The reformist/progressive "Imperial Republic of America" elected John Kennedy—its tragic "Camelot President." The USA, winners of the Cold War and the "space-race" (since "the Star Wars race" was never really implemented), had Ronald Reagan—the Teflon President. Now, the "America-to-be-made-great-again" chose to elect Donald Trump, the first "Casino-Owner-Real Estate-President," presiding over a New World order in which societies are formatted, informed, and monitored by a nexus of High-Tech apparatuses, informatics, the social media, and the "categorical imperative" to enjoy (Slavoj Zizek), itself intimately linked to an unfettered type of capitalism.

This is not really new. The periodic return in the popular Imaginary of the "1900s' Robber Baron capitalists"—considered "Empire-builders," the lingering ideological legacy of Ayn Rand's objectivism (reasoned selfishness and individualist pursuit of happiness), the totally un-regulated or de-regulated vision of a free-market espoused by the neo-con movement of the 1980s/1990s (which produced the crash of 2008), get "the government-off-my-back" Reaganist populist motto, the anti-Washingtonian credo of the Tea-Party movement…, all paved the way for new sentiments, beliefs, and convictions, which culminated in the election of Donald Trump. But there is something different in what will become known one day as Trumpism.

The new world order induces in people (the ex-proletarian masses, the multitude—Hardt/Negri, the individualist consumers…) a hyper-virtual literacy increasingly disconnecting the Symbolic from the Imaginary and the Real, to use Lacanian topology.

This loss of "the Symbolic tie" is not the product of a re-alignment/re-invention of a new Symbolic along different lines and yielding a new hierarchy or order of things. It is not radical in a "revolutionary meaning" because it is not a reversal of a socio-political order, by which an exploited class/race/nation overthrows the one which oppresses it. It is not the spin-off of an intellectual, philosophical program (Enlightenment for the French Revolution, Marxism for the Russian Revolution, anti-colonialism studies for Third World independence movements of the 1960s…).

Trump's populism is conservative because it does not really question the status quo, the way things are, or the world order (for instance, the ultra-capitalist exploitation or Wall Street domination). It is reactionary because it wants to roll back 50 years of social progress, despite 30 years of neo-con propaganda against such advances. It is reactive because it is short-sighted and betrays a knee-jerk type of infantile, spontaneous outburst. It favors "emotionalism," and trite sentimentalism (the type favored by the new hyper-literacy)—hence the constant use of expletives, offensive posturing, stereotyping, emphatic bombasts, metonymic mimicking and gimmicks.

This de-symbolization is merely "symbolic" and stops short of radical interventions—hence its preponderance of "attitudinal" behavior: disrespect for tradition, cultivation of scandalous gestures or undiplomatic utterances and speech-acts—it still is symptomatic of the postmodernity breakdown, in the sense that the Imaginary is given a freer rein and escapes the control of the Symbolic. This explains the return of a certain primary dimension in politics, where what psychoanalysis calls the *ideal ego* reigns supreme. It is also the symptom of what *Community at Loose Ends* explains, when both the New Left (or what is left of it) and the New Right (now the "alt-right") appeal to the same concept.[70]

It is paranoid because it manipulates and uses as a scapegoat the fear of difference—this very difference induced and exacerbated by mass waves of immigration and human trafficking (fluxes of documented or undocumented workers, exploited women or children produced by the demands of a rampant and uncontrolled capitalist globalization. The logic of capitalist surplus-value demands this exploitation of foreign labor via international wage competition or legal/illegal importation of cheap foreign labor. This ethnic/racial/religious difference favored by international capital, forced down the throats of workers under the name of competition, was made palatable to them (by multiculturalism, diversity, and hybridity), via international tourism, intellectual, artistic, scientific, educational and cultural exchanges and cooperation, cheaper consumer products (Walmart has done more to "de-radicalize the masses" than any other company, institution or ideology), ethnic food, etc. Capital became international (global), and its effects started to ripple-out. The crisis of 2008 put a damper on this seductive participation. There were signs of the limits to this enterprise, which was carried out under the aegis of a Pan-American culture. Although the art scene is now global (Calcutta, Mumbai, Shanghai, Dakar, Sao Paulo, are as important as New York, Paris, Berlin, London or Los Angeles) the screen presence or commercial distribution of foreign films (non-Hollywood or non-European) in the world, is limited (except for the video-distribution of national cinemas) which clearly indicates the cultural limits of such an internationalization of cultural exchanges. That is to say that this global, capitalist culture of international differences has limits. It tends to make national governments/ states irrelevant, make many countries poor participants or beneficiaries of the flux of consumption, international enlightenment, and increased well-being, and leave entire segments of their populations behind. Wall-Mart or Shopping-Mall cultures, or even "Multinational Corporate-Culture," for that matter, are poor substitutes for a genuine hybrid culture of international differences.

This global reification and commodification of exchanges which went viral and international, with a certain culture of difference, bringing this difference under the form of poor, destitute, culturally and religiously different immigrants at the doorsteps of the petit-bourgeois or the de-classed workers of Europe and America, aroused a backlash. The difference came back with the capitalist crisis via the wrong side of things (fear, rejection and hatred—i.e. paranoia), re-igniting the repressed, but always latent, racism of the populace.

The 20th century was marked by the struggle to the death between International Socialism (communism and socialism) and National-Socialism (itself an hysteric by-product of capitalism in its anti-capitalist struggle). Perhaps the 21st century will be marked by the struggle between International Capitalism and National Capitalism.

Trump's populism and its European counterparts are national capitalisms.

This New World Order arouses a new form of populism crisscrossed by contradictions, haunted and united by a common enemy: the threat of difference, outside and inside difference. Although anti-hierarchical, it respects power and money. Although pretending to defend the working class, it cannot expand its vision beyond the national borders. It misrecognizes its class-enemy, taking its Robber Barons as saviors and poor immigrants as adversaries. It is the incarnation par excellence of Marxian "false consciousness" and Lacanian mis-recognition and passion for ignorance.

Conclusion

It is a good thing to take on the despair of the marginalized, downtrodden white populations, of the people of the vacant-lot and back-alley neighborhoods, the forgotten and depressed of rural America, but why ignore the forgotten, downtrodden and impoverished others? Since the outrageous disparity between rich and poor bridges the social, racial and ethnic divides, and since anti-black racism exacerbates the inequalities on one side of the socio-economic divide, why did Trump ignore the special plight of the poor black communities and inner-city-ghettoes—except for a few derogatory "campaign comments" here and there and a lackadaisical "you have nothing to lose by voting for me"? This missing hole in Trump's discourse is ominously telling, especially when he knows, as does any American, the legacy of the tragic history America left on the shoulders of the black population. Why was he unable to address the suffering and suicidal despair of black ghettoes, like Bernie Sanders? The suffering of those who are shot when finding themselves on the wrong side of the militarized "thin blue line" which tries to keep the social chaos of poor communities from engulfing whole cities? The suffering of those who disproportionally fill the jails while the upper class fills fancy restaurants, museums, luxury resorts, and night-clubs?

There is something of the "Decline and Fall of

Rome" in the present spectacle of our affluent societies—something presciently illustrated by Godard's political films of the 70s, which gives this quote from Cicero's *Orations* an uncanny, prescient dimension:

"When, O Catiline, do you mean to cease abusing our patience? How long is that madness of yours still to mock us? When is there to be an end of that unbridled audacity of yours, swaggering about as it does now?...

Do you not feel that your plans are detected? Do you not see that your conspiracy is already arrested and rendered powerless by the knowledge which every one here possesses of it?...

Who was there that you summoned to meet you—what design was there which was adopted by you, with which you think that any one of us is unacquainted?

...

Shame on the age and on its principles! The senate is aware of these things; the consul sees them; and yet this man lives. Lives! aye, he comes even into the senate. He takes a part in the public deliberations; he is watching and marking down and checking off for slaughter every individual among us. And we, gallant men that we are, think that we are doing our duty to the republic if we keep out of the way of his frenzied attacks...

That destruction which you have been long plotting

against us ought to have already fallen on your own head...

You alone have had power not only to neglect all laws and investigations, but to overthrow and break through them...

Neither the guard who watches over the Palatine Hill at night, nor the posts spread in the city, nor the terror of the people, nor the concurrence of all the good citizens, nor the choice, for the meeting of the Senate, of this most sure place of all, neither the looks nor the faces of those who surround you, nothing disconcerts you? You do not feel that your projects are unveiled? You do not see that your conspiracy remains powerless, as soon as we all have the secret? Do you think that one of us does not know what you did last night and the night before, where you went, what men did you get together, what resolutions did you take?...

But we cannot expect that you should be concerned at your own vices, that you should fear the penalties of the laws, or that you should yield to the necessities of the republic, for you are not, O Catiline, one whom either shame can recall from infamy, or fear from danger, or reason from madness...

But if you have a fear of unpopularity, is that arising from the imputation of vigor and boldness, or that arising from that of inactivity and indecision most to be feared?"[71]

Is Donald Trump a conscious or unconscious peddler of racism (something which emerged in his past discourses, each time a Mediatized/notorious sexual crime was committed by a non-white) or did he choose to cater to the lowest sentiments of his electorate for opportunistic reasons? Playing "white lives matter," "blue lives matter," or "all lives matter" (the philistine cynical outcry), on against "black lives matter," and scapegoating minorities and people of color (especially immigrants) subverts any social "universalism" Trump's politics and policies pretend to espouse. His American form of populism mixed with a "nationalist capitalism" has an international appeal (other "nationalist populisms and capitalisms" whose guiding principles and goals were heralded by the ones of the English "Brexit") but within no universalist, social dimension. Trump's politics are not "national socialist" as opposed to "international socialist" but "national populist." Main-stream commentators declared that he even went so far as giving a voice to white supremacists in the Republican Party. His universal electoral denominator is the "common man and woman," who founded the Tea Party movement, not the exploited worker as such. Although no Dr. Mabuse, what Trump has unleashed comes from deep inside the American collective unconscious. [xv] It is a tidal wave (with rip current effects) of resentment fed by the energy of popular affects and effects resulting from deep-seated socio-economic woes. He is surfing this tsunami like a "golden beach-boy" à la Elvis Presley, for everybody to see, enjoying every minute of "It" (hence his constant allusions, often in inappropriate circumstances, to his popularity and the crowds who supposedly adore him). Whatever the "real Donald Trump" thinks or feels, his infantile, boasting political behavior (or lack of behavior), his constant use of simplistic dichotomies, his apparent incapacity to face up to the arcane complexity of the postmodern world in a meaningful manner, his lack of articulate and far-seeing proposals, do not augur well for his presidency. It is not so much that Trump's outbursts that are dangerous for our rights in the long run, as are his Supreme Court and Cabinet nominations. *"The Trump administration is off to the rockiest start of any presidency in recent history. Consumed by extreme paranoia, we have a president who routinely throws out radical, unsubstantiated accusations, sees spies behind every bush (or electronic device), and fears enemies foreign and domestic. Yet, 500 of the 522 presidential appointments to be confirmed by the Senate remain unfilled."*[72]

Only time will tell, although the national budget he proposed to Congress already provides ample matter for worry, pain and anguish in the future. If he and his Cabinet carry on the same path unopposed, five years from now America will be a very different country.

Donald Trump is at once a catalyst, a conduit, a lightning-rod, and an agent provocateur, which means that his exercise of presidential power and executive orders will require people to watch his policies closely and react quickly (as Senator Elizabeth Warren and others recommended after his election) in order to restrict any serious infringements he may commit upon the basic democratic rules that still govern us. The "black hole" and the "white flare" in Trump's discourse should motivate people who care about the future of America to redouble their efforts in obstructing the horrors which may result from an exacerbated, bi-polar, "black and white world," and from a society delivered without protection from the unleashed entrepreneurial capital of predators, speculators, "carpet baggers with laptops," "banksters," and traffickers of all sorts: i.e. the dictatorship of exploiters.

The thing not to do is to withdraw from the political scene, or drown one's sorrows in chagrin, despair, "artificial paradises," shopping, politically correct "safe-spaces," and/or one's own private island (business as usual). It is time to question and confront the desolation of the enjoyment of populists, our neighbors, colleagues, and fellow-citizens. Donald Trump's election must be a call-to-arms for all true democratic forces to stand up and be counted for the people, their rights and their welfare.

"At the apogee we beget values; at twilight, worn and defeated, we abolish them. Fascination of decadence—of the ages when the truths have no further life... when they pile up like skeletons in the dessicated, pensive souls, in the boneyard of dreams."[73]

NOTES

Endnotes

1   E.M. Cioran. *A Short History of Decay*. Arcade Publishing: 1998. 119.

2   Although ignoring the internationalist/nationalist political divide issuing from the Marxist explanation of class-warfare, the following *Economist* article provides a few insights into what is today called populism. *"DONALD TRUMP, the populist American president-elect, wants to deport undocumented immigrants. Podemos, the populist Spanish party, wants to give immigrants voting rights. Geert Wilders, the populist Dutch politician, wants to eliminate hate-speech laws. Jaroslaw Kaczynski, the populist Polish politician, pushed for a law making it illegal to use the phrase "Polish death camps." Evo Morales, Bolivia's populist president, has expanded indigenous farmers' rights to grow coca. Rodrigo Duterte, the Philippines' populist president, has ordered his police to execute suspected drug dealers. Populists may be militarists, pacifists, admirers of Che Guevara or of Ayn Rand; they may be tree-hugging pipeline opponents or drill-baby-drill climate-change deniers. What makes them all "populists," and does the word actually mean anything?*

Widespread use of the term "populism" dates to the 1890s, when America's Populist movement pitted rural populations and the Democratic Party against the more urban Republicans. (It was also used to refer to Russia's 19th-century narodnichestvo movement, which was largely comprised of self-hating intellectuals with a crush on the peasantry.) In the 1950s academics and journalists began applying it more broadly to describe everything from fascist and communist movements in Europe to America's anti-communist McCarthyites and Argentina's Peronistas. As Benjamin Moffitt explains in his book "The Global Rise of Populism," a conference at the London School of Economics in 1967 agreed that the term, while useful, was too mushy to be tied down to a single description. Some scholars linked it to frustration over declines in status or welfare, some to nationalist nostalgia. Others saw it as more of a political strategy in which a charismatic leader appeals to the masses while sweeping aside institutions (though not all populist movements have such a leader). Despite its fuzziness, the term's use has grown. In 2004 Cas Mudde, a political scientist at the University of Georgia, offered a definition that has become increasingly influential. In his view populism is a "thin ideology", one that merely sets up a framework: that of a pure people versus a corrupt elite. (He contrasts it with pluralism, which accepts the legitimacy of many different groups.) This thin ideology can be attached to all sorts of "thick" ideologies with more moving parts, such as socialism, nationalism, anti-imperialism or racism, in order to explain the world and justify specific agendas. Poland's Mr Kaczynski, a religious-nationalist populist, pushes for a Catholic takeover of his country's institutions from elite secular liberals. The Dutch Mr Wilders, a secular-nationalist populist, demands a crackdown on Islam (in defence of gay rights) and reviles the multicultural elite. Spain's Podemos, an anarchist-socialist populist party, pushes to seize vacant buildings owned by banks and distribute them to the poor, and attacks "la casta" (the elite caste).

This "thin ideology" definition of populism seems apt in Britain, where Brexiteers denounce experts, refer to themselves as "the people" and boast of having "smashed the elite". Indeed, Brexit seems to lack a unified "thick ideology": Brexiteers have different attitudes to trade, race, government spending and almost everything else. But other scholars feel that the thin-ideology definition fails to capture some dimensions. Jan-Werner Müller, a political scientist at Princeton University, thinks populists are defined by their claim that they alone represent the people, and that all others are illegitimate. And there are important distinctions within the category, such as that between inclusive and exclusive varieties. Exclusive populism focuses on shutting out stigmatized groups (refugees, Roma), and is more common in Europe. Inclusive populism demands that politics be opened up to stigmatized groups (the poor, minorities), and is more common in Latin America. Mr Mudde argues that while most writers deplore populism, its upside lies in forcing elites to discuss issues they prefer to ignore. But populism's belief that the people are always right is bad news for two elements of liberal democracy: the rights of minorities and the rule of law." (M.S. What is populism? In The Economist. Dec. 19, 2016).

3   Jean Baudrillard in *Simulacrum and Simulation*. U. of Michigan. 1994. 99.

4   Slavoj Zizek. *For They Know Not What They Do: Enjoyment As A Political Factor.* Verso Press, London/New-York: 1991, 2008. 270.

5   Ryan Foley. *Spread of Fake News Prompts Literary Efforts in Schools.* Associated Press. December 2017.

6   Jeffrey Geiger. *Special Relationships: British Higher Education and the Global Marketplace* in *PMLA. Special Topics: Literatures at Large.* January 2004. Vol. 119. # 1. 66,67.

7   See the work of the French sociologist and philosopher Jean Baudrillard.

8   *The New Colossus* is a sonnet written by American poet Emma Lazarus (1849–1887) in 1883 to raise money for the construction of the pedestal of the Statue of Liberty. In 1903, the poem was engraved on a bronze plaque and mounted inside the pedestal's lower level. As we all know, huge areas of plastic garbage (the new "refuse of our teeming shores") some as large as Texas, float around in the different oceans.

9   Read Nadia Urbinati and Arturo Zampaglione's *The Antiegalitarian Mutation: The Failure of Institutional Politics in Liberal Democracies.* Columbia University Press. 2016.

10   Argument used by the City of Missoula administration in order to legally force the Carlyle group to sell its Missoula Water company to the city for the paltry sum of $83 million

plus.

11   Herbert Marcuse. *"The Obsolescence of the Freudian Concept of Man"* in *Five Lectures.* Boston: Beacon Press, 1970. 44-61. Citation quoted by Laurence A. Rickels in *The Case of California.* University of Minnesota Press. 2001. 277.

12   Our world is ontologically, visually, ethically, and epistemologically dominated by capital. Century-old forms of political struggle (protests, demonstrations, unions, political parties, radical social and political critiques and movements…) increasingly take on the appearance and status of "curios" or objects of nostalgia. They may soon become artifacts worthy of commemorative re-enactments fairs (like "Renaissance" or "Medieval Fairs") where they will stage their own disappearance—what the sociologist Jean Badudrillard calls the "disappearance of politics." Joe Klein in *Time Magazine (*May 30 2016) writes that Trump *"is selling nostalgia bigtime" Make America Great…Again… In other words, he's done a stunning job of repurposing the past as the future. In the end, though, nostalgia is a sepiatoned refuge for those suffering a sense of diminished capacity—of wars, and manufacturing jobs lost, of father knows best, of racial privi-lege. It is a nursing home for those comfortable looking back than looking forward."*

13   Carolyn Chute's *The Beans of Egypt* is the most humane and understanding literary testimonial to the lives of "these undesirables."

14   There is a special, sub-cultural, mental hermeticism typical of the Great Plains. It is characterized by a lack of emotional depth and metaphoric verticality echoing, or mimicking—since an echo implies a vertical mass bouncing back the sound wave, the infinite flatness of the land where the horizon keeps receding forever. There, the human gaze overlooking the land is overwhelmed by its geographical immensity; it does not encounter any resistance and loses itself in an empty, big sky (although only its Eastern side

is part of the Great Plains, Montana is known as "Big Sky Country"). On these vast expanses, the only material proofs of physical verticality are the grain elevators (sometimes as high as cathedrals) or the domes of local courthouses. This peculiar state of mind exacerbates the pragmatism, matter-of-fact empiricism, and utilitarianism characterizing Anglo-Saxon capitalism. It entertains intellectual platitudes, flattens the poetic creative imagination, but favors technical creativity (there are a lot of "garage-tinkerers" and technical inventors in these States). When desperate for transcendence and depth, or simply yearning for an answer to their questioning inwardness, Great Plains' inhabitants compensate by investing themselves in extreme, emotional elations, irrational resentment, or "fantasmatic transports"—which explain the strange crimes, the extreme religious fervor and radical forms of rural populism popping up here and there, all over the land of infinite horizontality. David Lynch, in his *Twin Peaks* series, made a special use of this Great Plains' cultural hermiticism, by moving it to the regional context of the woods, mountains, and pulp-mills of the Rockies and Pacific Northwest.

15   *"As the gap between rich and poor grew wider after 2000, conservatives took the lead in white trash bashing."* Nancy Isenberg. *White Trash. The 400-Year Untold History of Class in America.* Penguin Books. 2016. 308.

16   Nancy Isenberg. Idem. xiv.

17   *"In the first two decades of the twentieth century, when the eugenics movement flourished, they were the class of degenerates targeted for sterilization. On the flip side, poor whites were the beneficiaries of rehabilitative efforts during the New Deal and in LBJ's "Great Society."* Nancy Isenberg. Idem. xvii.

18   Nancy Isenberg. Idem. 306.

19   The state of Montana (a rural red state which has voted for only two Democrats since 1952), has one of the highest

rate of alcoholism, D.U.I., and suicide in the nation.

20   Term used by French psychoanalysis to characterize extreme enjoyment, sexual pleasure, existential pleasure, and symptomatic pleasure (death-drive).

21   It is easy to understand how many populist, conspiracy theorists believe that the System is "out to get them" without coming out and saying that there is "somewhere" (at the "top of the food-chain") an "unspoken plan" to get rid of the "unnecessariat," the "expendables," i.e., the people who are a drain on the System, etc. To prove their paranoid belief, they point at the expensive health care system in America is designed to kill poor people. They are persuaded that the System is cynically and hypocritically Malthusian, because there is simply not "enough room at the table for everyone." A large swath of (mostly young) poor people (Blacks, Whites and Chicanos) are already pushed aside every year, losing their voting rights and all prospects for a "meaningful, normal life" thanks to the ideology and logic of the criminal justice system, and its offshoot, the prison system—which explains why the incarceration rate in the US is the highest in the world. They also cite "cheap food," or the way the distribution/consumption system is organized, which finishes off the "skin-job" via obesity, diabetes, cardiac diseases, etc.

22   The same drift towards the populist right is also affect-ing Europe—something well analyzed by many European political analysts and intellectuals. For instance, the German theatre director Thomas Ostermeier staged this year in New-York the "autobiographical essay" by the French philosopher Didier Eribon's play *Returning to Reims*, with Nina Hoss (from *Homeland*'s fame) as main actress. The play addresses the poignant drama of an intellectual who, upon going back home for a long visit, discovers that the liberal (European meaning) and left-leaning middle-class of his "child-hood-town" have all abandoned the working-class to its "globalist fate." Feeling ignored or disregarded even by the

different "partis de gauche" the workers ran in mass into the "saving arms" of the Front National. It seems that populism's march around the globe has put progressive political activism in a quandary.

23   Although there are entrepreneurs who have utopian visions like the CEOS of High-Tech companies such as Google, the dreams of these High-Tech gurus and pundits rarely imply a radical, pluralist democratization of our society. Their socio-political visions are more Roman than Athenian.

24   As Octave (played by Jean Renoir himself) ironically declares in *The Rules of the Game*, 1939.

25   Roland Barthes. *The Rustle of Language.* University of California Press, 1986. 45.

26   Slavoj Zizek. *The Sublime Object of Ideology.* Verso 2008. 15, 16.

27   *The Hightower Lowdown.* Volume 20, Number 2. February 2018.

28   *The Hightower Lowdown.* Volume 20, Number 2. February 2018.

29   Marx and Engels. *Communist Manifesto*. Millennium Publications. 2015. 49.

30   E.M. Cioran. *A Short History of Decay*. Arcade Publishing: 1998. 113.

31   To know more on the topic, consult Pacho Velez and Sierra Pettengill's *The Reagan Show*.

32   Hulk Hogan was the professional wrestler cast as the good hero fighting against corrupt leadership in Thomas Wright's action film *No Holds Barred*,1989.

33   Judd Legum. *This French philosopher is the only one who can explain the Donald Trump phenomenon* in *Thin Progress. September 2014.* It is about Roland Barthes' *Mythologies*

published in 1957 (Hill and Wang. 1972), and especially the chapter entitled *The World of Wrestling*.

34   "*The society of the spectacle*" (from the book with the same title by Guy Debord) corresponds to the social/societal stage of a late/advanced/decadent civilization when capital itself becomes not only its own spectacle, but also the one proposed to the masses via the Media and the screens of hyper-virtuality—or the "*panem and circenses*" of the late Roman Empire.

35   Roland Barthes. Idem. 15.

36   Roland Barthes. Idem. 21, 22.

37   Shakespeare. *Hamlet*. Hamlet "*to be or not to be*" soliloquy.

38   "*Perversion, Idealization and Sublimation*" in the *International Journal of Psycho-Analysis 55* (1974). 363.

39   Julia Kristeva. *Powers of Horror: An Essay on Abjection*. Columbia U. Press: 1982.1.

40   George Bataille. *The Psychological Structure of Fascism*. Trans. Carl R. Lovitt in *New German Critique*. No. 16 (Winter 1979). P. 66, 67, 69.

41   Julia Kristeva. *Powers of Horror: An Essay on Abjection*. Columbia U. Press: 1982. 3,4.

42   Fredric Jameson. *The Political Unconscious*. Cornell U. Press: 1981. Jameson analyzes narratives as socially symbolic acts (Marxist interpretation) as well as actions influenced by the unconscious (Freudian interpretation).

43   Slavoj Zizek. *Metastases of Enjoyment: Six Essays on Woman and Causality*. Verso Press: 1994.162.

44   Gilles Deleuze & Félix Guattari. *L'Anti-Oedipe: Capitalisme et Schizophrénie* (1972). Translated in English as *Anti-Oedipus: Capitalism and Schizophrenia* in 1989. 121.

45   The case of the Jewish presence (and persecution) in European societies works differently and cannot constitute a blueprint for the contemporary assimilation problem of "foreign others." Anti-Semitism has been the object of excellent studies.

46   Slavoj Zizek. *Refugees, Terror and Other Troubles with the Neighbors: Against the Double Blackmail.* Melville House: London. 2016. 37.

47   Slavoj Zizek. *The Neighbor.* U. of Chicago Press: 2005. 140.

48   Slavoj Zizek. *Idem.* 140.

49   Jean Baudrillard. *The Vital Illusion*, Columbia U. Press. 2000. 53.

50   Excerpt from an Editorial in *The Record* (Hackensack, New Jersey).

51   1978 American war-drama film co-written and directed by Michael Cimino. The diegesis revolves around a trio of American steelworkers (Robert De Niro, Christopher Walken and John Savage) whose lives are changed forever after serving in the Vietnam War—John Cazale (his last role) and Meryl Streep in supporting roles. The film takes place in the small mill-town of Clairton (south of Pittsburgh) and in Vietnam. The film is partly based on Louis Garfinkle and Quinn Redeker's screenplay *The Man Who Came to Play* about Las Vegas and Russian roulette. The producer Michael Deeley, who bought the story, hired writer/director Michael Cimino who, with Deric Washburn, rewrote the script, transposing the Russian roulette sequence to the American war in Vietnam.

52   Of course they conveniently ignore that America has the largest per capita military spending in the world. *"Trump's new budget calls for cutting social, family and senior services, education, environmental protection, and science budgets to*

throw an additional $54 billion annually into the black hole of the military-industrial complex. While our chest-pounder in chief lauds this "historic" military buildup, the simple truth is that we already out-spend all the other top military budgets in the world combined. So why should we further bloat our $2 billion-a-day military expenditures? Yet Democrats appear to be willing to go along with such fiscal idiocy – providing there are matching expenditures on domestic programs." George Ochenski. *Will Trump wage war with North Korea? Missoulian.* 3/20/2017.

53   See the work of the French philosopher Gilles Deleuze.

54   Something well explained by writers such as the journalist, "socio-naturalist" Frank Norris (*The Octopus: A Story of California*—1901), or the socio-realist Sinclair Lewis (*Babbit*—1922), and also by film noirs (one of the latest being Roman Polanski's *Chinatown*—1974).

55   Slavoj Zizek. *Refugees, Terror and Other Troubles with the Neighbors: Against the Double Blackmail.* Melville House. London:2016. 82.

56   Slavoj Zizek. *For they know not what they do: enjoyment as a political factor.* Verso Press: 1991. 2.

57   Ian Volner. *Fool's Gold* in *Artforum,* Nov. 2016.

58   Quoted by Ian Volner. *Fool's Gold* in *Artforum,* Nov. 2016. Ian Volner alludes to the now famous aphorism *"I am a monument"* coined by Venturi to illustrate his brand of postmodernism in his influential and controversial architecture manifesto written with Denise Scott Brown and Steven Izenour, *Learning from Las Vegas*, published by the MIT Press in 1972.

59   Idem. 241.

60   In ancient times, the letter T (tau), 19th letter of the Greek alphabet, derived from the last letter of the Phoenician alphabet (the letter X), was used for symbolizing life

and resurrection. In Biblical times, the "tau" or "taw" was attached to men to distinguish those who lamented sin—whose symbolic function was similar, although antithetically, to the scarlet letter "A" Hester Prynne had to wear on her dress in the Puritan Boston of 1642 (Hawthorn's novel of 1850). The symbolism of the cross was connected not only to the letter X (chi) but also to T (tau), like the last letter of the Old Hebrew alphabet. It was originally cruciform in shape (Cross of Tau, which had the shape of the crucifixes used by the Romans). An essay written around 160 AD, attributed to Lucian, a mock legal prosecution called *The Consonants at Law — Sigma v. Tau in the Court of Seven Vowels* contains a reference to the cross attribution. Sigma petitions the court to sentence Tau to death by crucifixion, saying: *"Men weep, and bewail their lot, and curse Cadmus with many curses for introducing Tau into the family of letters; they say it was his body that tyrants took for a model, his shape that they imitated, when they set up structures on which men are crucified.* Stauros *(cross) the vile engine is called, and it derives its vile name from him. Now, with all these crimes upon him, does he not deserve death, nay, many deaths? For my part I know none bad enough but that supplied by his own shape — that shape which he gave to the gibbet named* stauros *after him by men."* Does Trump carries his I on his rump?

61   *"The lady doth protest too much, me thinks."* says the Queen to Hamlet (Act 3, Scene 2).

62   Edmund Spencer, 1590.

63   Anatoly Liberman. *Ostentatious breeches, Gods' braggadocio, and arspoetica* in *Word Origins*.

64   He is "*it*" would put him on the female side of the *sexuation graph*, a Lacanian would say.

65   These affinities go beyond the legacies of the ex-USA/USSR-past-divide and resist the recent resurgence of American neo-McCarthyism in America. Trump's conception of

what America should be and Putin's vision for Russia seem to share some affinities in regard to populism and their no- tions of what "national capitalism" should be. Russian popu- lism and nationalism are closely tied to Russian Eurasianism, a Pan-Slavic geo-political and military doctrine, first put together by Aleksandr Dugin, ex-Chair of the Department of Sociology of International Relations at Moscow State University. Dugin used a syncretism of different socio-cul- tural, historical, and political elements to forge a doctrine which influenced the geostrategic vision of Vladimir Putin's administration (Pan-Slavism). Often associated with National Bolshevism, Eurasianism opposes international capitalism while rejecting the internationalism of the Soviet-style of Bolshevism (such as Trotskyism). Eurasianism is Pan-Rus- sian of course, and promotes Orthodox spirituality. It bases its foreign policies on a systematic opposition to the Ameri- can-led New World Order and a USA-controlled Europe.

Eurasianism is anti-globalist, anti-Western, anti-Atlantic, and anti-NATO (since NATO is the corner stone of the Ameri- ca-dominated-West from a Russian perspective). Eurasianist strategists and geo-politicians consider the "Pan-American/ Western Alliance" to be a socio-political and economic nexus of forces whose sole purpose is to create a global, West- ern-based, political and cultural hegemony. By submerging nations and religions within the fluxes and flows of a single neo-capitalist economic system (globalization as *pensée unique*—a single, one-way type of economically thinking the world), Eurasianists think that the Western-based type of globalization is transforming the whole world into a mock-up of the West. They are convinced that, by transforming the whole world into a Western type of society, globalization produces and re-enforces Western hegemony, leaving no place for alternative economies or different socio-political systems. Voltaire wrote that *"In the beginning God created man in His own image, and man has been trying to repay the favor ever since."* The same loop, closed circle, or vicious circle of cause and effect can be said about capitalism and the world. As the French situationist Guy Debord states in *The Society of the Spectacle,* the capitalist economy is, of course, transforming the world (no doubt about it); but it is turning the world into a "capitalist world" of economy, re-making it according to the reductionist paradigms of capitalism. Eurasianists consider the European Union guilty of the "same sin," for projecting an aggressive libertarian (European meaning), secular and anti-religious image (i.e. its own image) on Europe's nations, and expecting them to fit and become that image, forgetting their own specificities and particular cultures. In this scenario, the E.U. is seen as having unwittingly awakened fundamentalist terrorisms. Eurasianists deplore the logic of the E.U. which pushes for a European super-state aiming at encompassing all Eastern European countries (which used to be in the Pan-Russian zone of influence) and suppressing national cultures and autonomies—hence the Eurasianists' approval of Brexit. Consequently, Eurasianism aims at forming alliances across the globe to counter globalization and Western/Atlantic hegemony with anti-globalist forces notwithstanding their political, national, religious, ethnic or cultural affiliations. The goal is to resist globalization and secure the economic, socio-political and cultural interests of the Nations opposed to this hegemony by constituting anti-Western, anti-globalization alliances. Leftist, nationalist, traditionalist forces opposed to globalization are courted in order to be included in these alliances. Eurasianism has an anti-capitalist dimension, or at least an anti-late-capitalist, or anti-neo-capitalist stand (according to the evolution of capitalism itself), since capitalism is associated with globalization. Eurasian Populism proposes a combination of advanced technology, spiritualism (religions), and anti-international capitalism.

Military and political ideologies are at the center of this diplomacy and doctrine. Eurasianism is a virulent and aggressive oppositional movement which wants to go viral and international. But since wars and battles are not what they used to be (they went through the same capitalist and High-Tech de-construction, de-territorialization, and de-lineariza-tion that changed the other sectors of societies), Eurasianist logistics, tactics and strategy are very postmodern. They are products of today's world, although they try to hang on to politico-historical elements/concepts and socio-cultural artifacts from the past. That is to say that to gain influence and counter Western globalist hegemony, Eurasianists think that wars do not have to be declared as such, any longer. Confrontations do not necessarily imply full-fledged battles as such. Instead, they are replaced by subversion, disin-formation, (counter-)manipulation, computer hacking and highjack, electronic systems' disruptions, etc.

Putin and Trump's policies seem to share beliefs and convic-tions. This may explain the so-called Russian "interferences" or "influences" in Donald Trump's presidential elections. Eurasianists welcome Trump's appeal and response to American populism, as well as his emphasis on national capitalisms—wherever they are. By working together, they think that American and Russian populisms can delineate their own spheres of influence in the world, especially in view of the rise of China as global, world power. Eurasianists welcome the potential dis-engagement, or at least partial re-treat of Trump's America from world affairs (new American isolationism) contained in his vague foreign policy doctrines. They welcome his understanding of "Real Politics" and his respect for strength and authoritarian governments, as well as his re-building a super-strong American military. Although new, the Eurasianist doctrine possesses many "problematic" left-overs from a past era. At the core of this doctrine, one finds the remnants of a dozing, or forgotten, more or less repressed (Soviet-like) ideology. It has returned and became resurrected, re-energized, and has surged back under a new patina. Projected on the future, it comes back from the past to haunt us. Obviously, bygones are not entirely bygones.

The populism of Eurasianism wants to fuse together a "social nationalism," or a "socialism with nationalism" (government planned economy), with an organic type of society based on spiritual dimensions. The Russian National Bolshevik Party (founded in 1992), later banned by Moscow, espouses this Eurasian doctrine. The National Bolshevik Party mixes communist and fascist symbolism, uniforms, and socio-political elements, which makes it suspect of harboring totalitarian elements, and even a strong fascistic dimension, reminiscent of the fascisms of the 1920s and 1903s until WWII dramatically shut off their blossoming. The organic dimension of the state, the use of root-spirituality (established religions), the ideological use of the land and religion (terrain and terroir), the Xenophobic and anti-Semitic elements, the cult of a viriloid type of aggressive posturing and socio-cultural behavior ("primary type" of phallocentrism incarnated by Donald Trump and Vladimir Putin), the cult of a strong military, a crude nationalism manipulating the socio-economic frustrations of the masses, the manipulation of the delinquent elements of society, the systemic cultivation of a nationally-based type of capitalism and economy…, a nationalism opposed to all internationalisms, all the signs of a "fascistoid" dimension are here. They all betray a nostalgia for a bygone era, which is re-emerging through the skin of the system, of society (its "pores" would Walter Benjamin say, or its "molecular lines" the French philosopher Deleuze would add…). They also characterize the different types of national populisms and alt-right movements, which have popped up all over the place and are right now trying to re-configure the Nation-State as well as the World. They move in the void created by the retreat and disappearance of the Left.

66   Jean Beaudrillard. *The Vital Illusion.* Columbia U Press, 2000. 15.

67   In *User's Guide to Capitalism and Schizophrenia: Deviations from Deleuze and Guattari.* M.I.T. Press, 1993. 131

68   Michael Milken is a former financier and philanthropist. He revolutionized Wall-Street through the extensive use of high-yield bonds ("junk bonds"). Following an "insider trading" investigation, he was convicted in 1989 after he pleaded guilty to felony charges for violating U.S. securities laws and for racketeering and securities fraud. As the result of a plea bargain, he pleaded guilty to securities and reporting violations but not to racketeering or "insider trading." Milken was sentenced to ten years in prison, fined $600 million, and permanently barred from the securities industry by the Securities and Exchange Commission. His sentence was reduced to two years after he cooperated in testifying against his former colleagues and for good behavior. His critics cited him as the epitome of Wall Street greed during the 1980s, and nicknamed him the "Junk Bond King."

69   Fritz Lang's film, *Dr. Mabuse, der Spieler*, 1922 and *Das Testament des Dr. Mabuse*, 1933—from Norbert Jacques' novels about a mad doctor who manipulates people into committing crimes.

70   Edited by the Miami Collective. University of Minnesota Press. 1991.

71   M. Tullius Cicero. *Cicero's Orations*, literally translated by C. D. Younge. Fine Editions Press, London, New York, 1856/1957. Pages 3, 10, 11, 13. Quotes brought to my attention by Christyann Brown, an artist and dance-therapist who lives in Missoula, Montana.

72   George Ochenski. *Will Trump wage war with North Korea?Missoulian*. 3/20/2017.

73   E.M. Cioran. *A Short History of Decay*. Arcade Publishing: 1998. 115.

Michel Valentin

Michel Valentin is a North American critical theorist who specializes in the understanding of culture and society through the tools of contemporary psychoanalysis. He is retired Professor of French at the University of Montana, and is currently on the faculty at the Existential Psychoanalytic Institute & Society.

More from EPIS Press

Zero Point

Critical Existential Psychoanalysis

    Dr. Kevin Boileau

Essays on Phenomenolgy and the Self

    Dr. Kevin Boileau

Prolegomenon Toward A Primate Rights Bill

    Dr. Kevin Boileau

Radio Conversations Concerning Design:
Volume 4, Part I

    Dr. Kevin Boileau & Nazarita Goldhammer

Other

On the Origin of the Self

    Loray Daws, PhD

About EPIS Press

We established EPIS Press in the objective of publishing new work in the following areas of inquiry:

1) existential psychoanalysis & phenomenology;

2) traditional & contemporary psychoanalysis theoretical and clinical;

3) critical philosophy as it pertains to psychoanalysis, culture, phenomenology, and philosophy of mind;

4) new literature in phenomenology and psychoanalysis;

5) any related work as it bears on these issues, including neuropsychology and psychoanalysis.

For more information go to
EPIS Press
2026 S. 9th W., #4
Missoula, MT 59801
epispublishing1@gmail.com
www.episworldwide.com